PRAISE FOR PHILLIS M
AND *RESILIENCE IN CONFLICT*

Having worked with Phillis Morgan at several training seminars for federal managers, I've been impressed with how she was able to inspire folks with years of management experience to open themselves up to the concept and practice of mindfulness. Now that she has written this book, I am pleased that a new and wider population of managers will benefit from her insights learned through years of research and experience. By laying out a step-wise mindfulness-based process that anyone can follow, she is helping managers foster workplace relationships that are stronger and will allow for higher quality decisions that do not allow fear of conflict to get in the way. Phillis has provided managers with a blueprint for success when confronting conflict in the workplace. We are in her debt.

—TODD V. WELLS
Executive Director, Federal Managers Association

Managing conflict well starts with managing ourselves well—how we think about, feel about, and respond to conflict. In her wonderfully innovative book, *Resilient in Conflict*, Phillis Morgan, J.D., embraces this concept fully, and using mindfulness practices provides a practical, easy-to-understand and useful guide for leaders and managers of any organization to engage conflict with more clarity, awareness, intention, and "resilience." An insightful read.

—RAY KRAMER
Adjunct professor of Clinical Law, New York University Law School

Written with candor and conviction, *Resilient in Conflict* is a must-read for any leader looking for ways to address workplace conflict from the inside-out. Phillis Morgan's insightful narrative addresses the tension that comes with conflict, and offers powerful prescriptions for developing confidence, self-insight, and resilience. A wonderful storyteller, Phillis delivers that rare combination of mindset development, skill acquisition, and lessons to develop the catalysts needed to become a more skillful leader when it comes to conflict and other difficult situations. I am grateful to Phillis for putting her life's work into the universe and have made the book required reading in my Emotional Intelligence classes.

—CHUCK GARCIA

Founder of The Emotional Intelligence Lab and Columbia University Professor

As people are invited to bring more of their whole selves into the workplace and public domain, the changes will be unsettling for many and conflicts are sure to arise. Leaders need to be prepared with new tools and a new perspective to navigate this shifting landscape. Through a three-decade career working with the highest levels of government and corporate America, Phillis Morgan lays out a practical approach for leaders to bring mindfulness to confront the opportunities workplace conflicts present.

—JASON BRIEFEL

Director of Policy & Outreach, Senior Executives Association

Phillis Morgan has a clear vision of a healthy workplace—it is one where managers don't run from conflict. She incorporates mindfulness practices as an essential path for not only moving beyond the fear of conflict, but also learning to accept it with courage. I've had the great pleasure of working with Phillis on live presentations as well as on her previous book. She never runs from challenges. She embraces them. And this spirit of embracing that which we find challenging I am confident will enliven leaders, managers, and supervisors who read this book.

—DAN GEPHART

Training Director/Editor

Resilient
─── IN ───
Conflict

HOW MANAGERS USE MINDFULNESS TO NAVIGATE
WORKPLACE CONFLICT WITH COURAGE

Resilient

—— IN ——

Conflict

HOW MANAGERS USE MINDFULNESS TO NAVIGATE
WORKPLACE CONFLICT WITH COURAGE

PHILLIS MORGAN, J.D.

Advantage®

Published by Advantage, Charleston, South Carolina.
Member of Advantage Media Group.

ADVANTAGE is a registered trademark, and the Advantage colophon is a trademark of Advantage Media Group, Inc.

Printed in the United States of America.

10 9 8 7 6 5 4 3 2 1

ISBN: 978-1-64225-399-3 (PB), 978-1-64225-468-6 (eBook)
LCCN: 2022903118

Cover design by Carly Blake.
Layout design by Mary Hamilton.

This publication is designed to provide accurate and authoritative information in regard to the subject matter covered. It is sold with the understanding that the publisher is not engaged in rendering legal, accounting, or other professional services. If legal advice or other expert assistance is required, the services of a competent professional person should be sought.

Advantage Media Group is proud to be a part of the Tree Neutral® program. Tree Neutral offsets the number of trees consumed in the production and printing of this book by taking proactive steps such as planting trees in direct proportion to the number of trees used to print books. To learn more about Tree Neutral, please visit www.treeneutral.com.

Advantage Media Group is a publisher of business, self-improvement, and professional development books and online learning. We help entrepreneurs, business leaders, and professionals share their Stories, Passion, and Knowledge to help others Learn & Grow. Do you have a manuscript or book idea that you would like us to consider for publishing? Please visit advantagefamily.com.

To the people managers. You are braver than you know.

CONTENTS

ACKNOWLEDGMENTS

My heartfelt thanks go to the many who have with loving kindness and generosity been guides as I've navigated the wisdom path, whose guidance has so influenced the spirit of this book, including Lama Zopa Rinpoche, Geshe Graham Woodhouse, Geshe Ngawang Rabga, Ven. Thubten Khadro, and yogi Shiva Rea. Sincere thanks as well for the many who have given assistance, in ways big and small, including all the members of the Advantage|Forbes team, Carlos Carmona, Catina Ellis, Christine Agnith, Crystal Mitchell Moten, Cynthia Clinton-Brown, Denise Thompson, Edie Brumskill, Edmund Burke, Kelly Bingham, Kimberly Johnson, Melvin Barnett, Monica Knight, Pauline Ahmad, Rafael Reyes, Richard Rosenthal, Robert Roehrich, Sheila Lawson, Sherri Anderson-Beasley, Stacia Harrje, Stephanie Bragglee, Tonya Abrams, Valerie Kimbro, Wanda Donnelly, and Yuriy Mikmaylov.

INTRODUCTION

You cannot control the results, only your actions.

—ALLAN LOKOS, MEDITATION TEACHER

I know intimately what it's like to feel that you are wrongly accused in the workplace. There is denial, anger, and disbelief. The feelings are like going through the stages of grief. And in a way, this makes sense, because being accused of wrongdoing entails a certain death of the image you have of yourself as a manager. The thoughts of who you thought you were and how you thought others perceived you are gone.

Many years before I began to study and practice mindfulness, I was a federal government manager supervising a small office. One of my employees accused me of sexual harassment. Eventually, with the full faith and support of my superiors, I was exonerated of the charge.

But as I endured the humiliation while I was dragged through the process of clearing my name, I was the poster child for poor emotional management. At times I felt anger that was so alive and present, it felt like something tangible. I was the model of righteous indignation during my interview with investigators, even though I knew quite well—I was an employment lawyer, after all—that such a demeanor would not help me. I simply couldn't help myself. Had the accusation not been so clearly outrageous, my reactions and behavior could have seriously undermined my case. Thus, I understand the challenges in regulating our emotional selves during conflict. It's not easy, but it's so very necessary.

Statistically, there's a good chance any people manager will be involved in some sort of employment lawsuit. According to the liability insurer Chubb, employment-practice lawsuits alleging discrimination, retaliation, and sexual harassment are some of the most common types of liability lawsuits companies and organizations face today.[1]

Other types of workplace conflicts are more common than lawsuits. Maybe you had an argument with a colleague. Perhaps a direct report responded aggressively to your feedback. Maybe your boss yelled at you for some perceived or real failure.

There are a number of causes of interpersonal workplace conflict, including the following:

» Clashing egos/personalities

» Cultural/values differences

» Differing work styles

» Poor communication

» Stress

In no cases do the encounters feel good.

Few people feel comfortable dealing with conflict. It evokes a range of reactions, from a sense of being under attack to feeling vulnerable and in the spotlight, from frustration and anger to fear. And such feelings are often expressed in our bodies. We may experience bodily sensations such as tension, flushed face, clenched hands, knotted stomach, or a tight chest, shoulders, jaw, neck, or head. If you feel resignation or even surrender, these feelings may be expressed by a slumped posture.

Often, a continuous internal dialogue accompanies the conflict. What did you say to yourself during the last conflict? Do you remember? Perhaps you made up a story about the object of unpleasantness or "source" of the trouble: "He's such an idiot. He never understands my instructions, and when things go south, he always deflects blame." Maybe you told a story about yourself: "Why am I always the one who has these discussions? I don't have time for this. Can't they see how busy I am?"

Did you feel you had the skills and confidence to handle the conflict? Even if you did not resolve the conflict, did you at least feel a sense of control over your emotional response? Probably not. Many managers—many people—receive little training in how to handle conflict. Without training, you can expect to feel ill-equipped to handle the situation, to lack confidence, and to feel overwhelmed by your emotions.

Even if you participated in training, most programs and workshops pay little attention to the role emotions play in conflict. All the techniques in the world won't help if you experience a sense of existential threat. When conflict makes you feel that your sense of self is in danger, it can shift the balance between intellect and emotion and hamper your ability to choose wise actions. When emotions gain the upper hand, they can spark, prolong, or exacerbate workplace conflict. Yet when was the last time you took a leadership development course in emotion management?

Interpersonal Conflict Catalysts

Emotional intelligence courses teach us about the critical role of emotions in building trust and respect, promoting collaboration, and promoting better, more innovative solutions. Yet many of these programs don't teach us how to identify and regulate our emotions.

Suppressing emotions, or trying to get rid of them altogether, isn't the answer. We need emotions; they play a critical role in survival. Emotions move us toward people and things that help us establish connection and nourish us, like the love of a mother or father for a child or the joy of engaging in meaningful work. And they help us avoid people and things that are threatening and harmful, like abusive spouses, the wrong career, or narcissistic bosses.

But confronted with conflict, typically we react unconsciously and perceive our emotions as overwhelming and possessing us instead of serving us. Because we have so little training in emotion regulation, this sense of overwhelm is frightening and leaves us feeling inadequately prepared to deal with emotion-laden conflict. As a result, our highly emotional states propel us to avoid conflicts or act in ways that exacerbate or prolong them. This is not good for the manager, employee, or organization.

The Costs of Workplace Conflict

I have more than three decades of experience as a labor and employment lawyer, working with the US government's largest employers as well as Fortune 100 companies. I have also worked with policy makers in Afghanistan, legal aid workers in Uganda, and legal scholars and entrepreneurs in Nepal. In my work I have seen the prohibitive costs of conflict to individuals, organizations, and countries. I have experienced firsthand how small problems become big ones because of the fear of dealing with conflict. This fear of conflict contributes to mission failure, further erosion of the relationship, and contributes to legal actions, putting billions of dollars, missions, and reputations at risk. The costs of conflict in the workplace are significant and include litigation, organizational and monetary costs, and physical and emotional costs. The types of litigation include discrimination actions, labor disputes, whistleblowing, and retaliation cases. Poorly managed and unmanaged conflict manifests in some of the most damaging ways for workers and their organizations. Every organization should strive to bring every reasonable strategy to bear to tackle workplace conflict. The costs of doing otherwise are too high.

This fear of conflict contributes to mission failure, further erosion of the relationship, and contributes to legal actions, putting billions of dollars, missions, and reputations at risk.

Lawsuits are one of the most damaging ways mismanaged conflict expresses itself. These include discrimination actions, labor disputes, whistleblowing, and retaliation cases. For example, in my experience, the overwhelming majority of discrimination complaints involve a dynamic that has more to do with clashing egos and personalities and less to do with discriminatory actions. To be clear, employment discrimination is not dead, and workers continue to experience discrimination in the workplace. It is also clear that, often, employees never report such actions for fear of retaliation or other harm. But the data show, and my experience affirms, that the vast majority of employment discrimination cases that are registered as formal complaints involve a nondiscriminatory conflict dynamic.

Even though organizations may prevail in a lawsuit, the costs to defend such lawsuits are significant.[2] More important and more salient than the dollar cost is the damage to workers' cohesion, trust, engagement, and productivity that flows from litigation. Lawyers take aggressive measures to vigorously represent and defend their clients. As a consequence, your time as a manager and your employees' time will be devoured by scouring through old files to find relevant documents, being interviewed or deposed, and responding to discovery questions. The litigation diverts time and attention from the organization's core mission. It airs the organization's dirty laundry: unsavory facts are shared and spread like wildfire throughout the organization, to customers, and to the public at large. The #MeToo movement is an excellent example of how social media publicizes and amplifies disputes that, in the past, may have largely remained internal and hidden from public view. Organizations are subjected to embarrassment, ridicule, and public collective action such as boycotts.

Employees team up and take sides. Who's for the company? Who's for the complainant? Judgments are rendered in the court of employee opinion. The manager was in the wrong, and employees may try to avoid her or withhold their best efforts when working with her. Or employees decide that the complainant is lying and may ostracize him. Feelings are hurt. Individual and institutional reputations are damaged. Employees quit rather than continue to be mired in unresolved conflict. Work areas may be restructured to separate employees, requiring the moved employee to learn new tasks and work culture and develop new working relationships. (Caution: Moving employees after a discrimination complaint has been filed may be improper. You should get legal advice before undertaking such an action.) Morale plummets and productivity declines. Who can work effectively amid all this strife?

Managers spend between 20 percent and 40 percent of their time dealing with conflict. Of course, not all of this time is unproductive. Some of it is well spent if the manager is engaged in actions meant to help manage and resolve the dispute. Productive actions include clarifying the issues, exploring options, and developing solutions. More typical, however, is spending the manager's and employee's time unproductively because of a fear of dealing directly with the conflict.

Regardless of whether poorly handled conflict results in lawsuits or informal complaints, managers, complainants, and other employees caught up in the conflict drama bear an emotional and physical cost. This manifests as stress, anxiety, hypervigilance, loss of trust, even post-traumatic stress disorder. Employees feel angry and frustrated when conflict is not being resolved, and these emotions extend to others for not resolving it. Complaining parties take more sick days and for longer periods due to the stress and anxiety that come with the complexity and vulnerability of accusing others and upsetting the status quo. Managers also experience stress and anxiety from being accused of moral failures or illegal actions and spend mental and emotional energy reviewing and second guessing their decisions. (Of course, such feelings are warranted if, in fact, the manager engaged in such wrongdoing.) Employees enmeshed in conflict lose commitment to the job, spend less time at work, and decrease their effort.

ORGANIZATIONAL COSTS OF CONFLICT

» Absenteeism

» Attrition

» Homogenous decisions

» Litigation

» Reduced motivation and commitment

» Reduced productivity

» Strife and mistrust

Potential Benefits of a Confident Approach to Conflict

What would happen if you could feel more confident in approaching conflict rather than avoiding it? With that greater confidence, what might conflict or disagreement help you achieve?

It's important to recognize that not all conflict is bad. Imagine a workplace without any conflict that arises from differences in world-views, experience, perceptions, attitudes, and the like. Such homogeneity, while perhaps easing interpersonal workplace friction, comes at a cost, including poorer quality of decisions and less innovation.

Conflict, then, can be productive. According to psychologists Sal Capobianco and Mark David, both faculty members at Eckerd College, and court and family mediator Linda Kraus, some potential benefits of approaching conflict effectively range from improving creativity and collaboration to enabling higher-quality decision making and implementation, all of which contribute significantly to organizational success. Companies that succeed at innovation support the robust debate of issues because it enables people to collaboratively generate chains of ideas and develop a comprehensive view of projects, products, customers' needs, and solutions to problems. Discussing competing ideas can involve conflict, and successfully working through conflict makes use of everyone's expertise and creativity.

BENEFITS OF EFFECTIVE APPROACHES TO CONFLICT

» Enhanced decision quality

» Improved motivation, commitment, productivity

» More creative decisions

» Reduced absenteeism, attrition, litigation, strife

» Stronger collaboration

» Stronger personal relationships

» Improved creativity

» Increased innovation

» Greater gains from diversity

» Better collaboration

» Enhanced decision quality

» Superior implementation

» Stronger relationships among stakeholders

In a workplace with people from diverse backgrounds—and this is increasingly the case as globalization affects increasing numbers of organizations—misunderstandings may arise because of cultural or language differences. Yet this diversity leads to varied perspectives and competing ideas and, therefore, more creative and innovative decisions. Effectively engaging in and resolving misunderstanding arising from diversity can lead to high-performing work groups and the organizations they are part of.

Effective conflict management can help build stronger relationships with clients and vendors, among employees, and between managers and employees. Successfully working through problems helps strengthen relationships, builds confidence that future problems can be effectively tackled, and helps make the work environment less stressful and more enjoyable.

In my consulting work, I see people avoiding conflict far more often than managing it skillfully. People keep what they think to themselves and do not share their opinions, fearing what might happen instead of collaboration.

All the knowledge about costs and benefits in the world, however, won't help if you do not have the skills to manage your emotions and behavior in the face of conflict. If you recall the story I told at the beginning of the introduction, I knew that anger and righteous indignation would not serve me well, yet I could not help myself. If we're poor at emotional regulation—and I include myself here—how do we break out of emotional reactions during conflict? If we haven't had training in emotional regulation, how do we break into a more effective approach that minimizes the costs and opens the door to benefits? The answer is to build our capacity for standing in the storm of conflict with greater resilience and wisdom.

Building the Capacity to Face Conflict with Resilience, Confidence, and Wisdom

Although we all have the capacity to step back from our emotions and choose our responses and actions wisely, none of us is born with these skills. Sometimes we learn them in the school of life, but sometimes the lessons are elusive. To learn these skills, we need to pay attention to our thoughts, emotions, and behaviors as they occur and reflect about the results we get. These attentions and reflections are challenging because we spend a lot of time in a kind of trance, engaged with thoughts about what we should have done or fears about the future.

A more direct approach is to engage in a program to build these mental and emotional muscles, much as you would work with a trainer at the gym or a running coach. And a more effective approach is to build the skills one step at a time, similar to how your first run would be a mile, not a marathon.

This book introduces, explains, and helps you work with the SNAP BC™ Method, a stepwise process that helps us build the mental and emotional muscles for working with conflict with greater resilience and confidence. It is a process for developing awareness and a mindful approach that helps us to snap out of unconscious and reactionary ways of responding to conflict. The approach addresses the domains of self-awareness, self-regulation, and adaptability. SNAP BC helps build competency in these domains, shown to be important in intelligently managing emotions. See the following Mindful Management of Self in Conflict graphic.

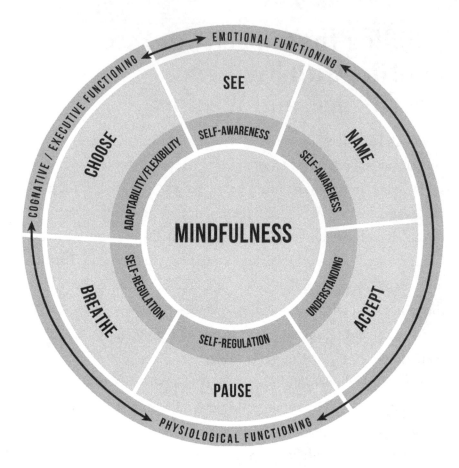

The acronym SNAP BC stands for See It (S), Name It (N), Accept It (A), Pause (P), Breathe (B), and Choose It (C). Each of the following chapters explains an element of the method and gives multiple ways to practice the skill involved and prepare to use it during conflict. Exercises enable you to engage with the techniques in real time, and then I show you how to use the technique during a conflict situation. Some chapters include additional exercises to help support these practices.

My goal for this book is to empower managers to learn how to better manage themselves while in conflict in the workplace. Using mindfulness as the principle tool, the aim is for managers to navigate workplace conflict with greater self-awareness, self-regulation, under-standing, and adaptability. In this way, managers can move from a place of reactivity, where conflict decisions lead to destructive organizational outcomes—such as reduced commitment and increased absenteeism—to a place of resilience, where decisions are characterized by greater insight and wisdom, in turn contributing to healthier organizational outcomes, including stronger relationships and enhanced decision quality. The SNAP BC approach is the path that will take you there.

Managing the Self in Conflict— BEFORE

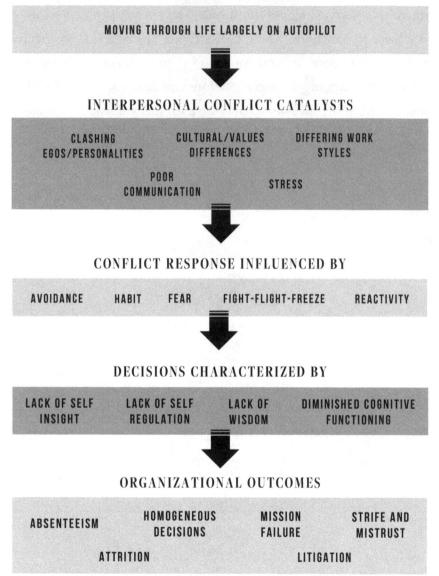

PREPARATION

MOVING THROUGH LIFE LARGELY ON AUTOPILOT

INTERPERSONAL CONFLICT CATALYSTS

CLASHING EGOS/PERSONALITIES

CULTURAL/VALUES DIFFERENCES

DIFFERING WORK STYLES

POOR COMMUNICATION

STRESS

CONFLICT RESPONSE INFLUENCED BY

AVOIDANCE   HABIT   FEAR   FIGHT-FLIGHT-FREEZE   REACTIVITY

DECISIONS CHARACTERIZED BY

LACK OF SELF INSIGHT

LACK OF SELF REGULATION

LACK OF WISDOM

DIMINISHED COGNITIVE FUNCTIONING

ORGANIZATIONAL OUTCOMES

ABSENTEEISM

HOMOGENEOUS DECISIONS

MISSION FAILURE

STRIFE AND MISTRUST

ATTRITION

LITIGATION

Managing the Self in Conflict— AFTER

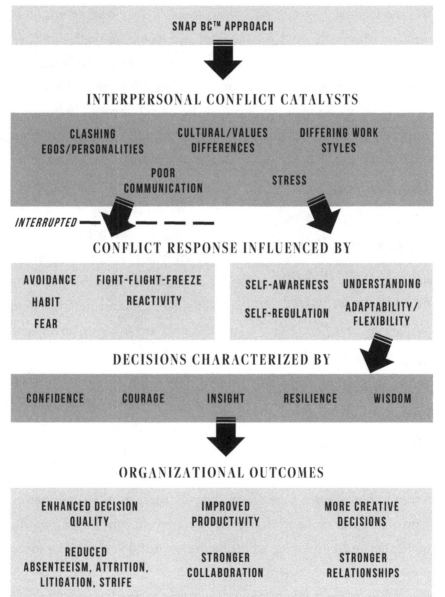

PREPARATION

SNAP BC™ APPROACH

INTERPERSONAL CONFLICT CATALYSTS

CLASHING
EGOS/PERSONALITIES

CULTURAL/VALUES
DIFFERENCES

DIFFERING WORK
STYLES

POOR
COMMUNICATION

STRESS

INTERRUPTED

CONFLICT RESPONSE INFLUENCED BY

AVOIDANCE   FIGHT-FLIGHT-FREEZE
HABIT   REACTIVITY
FEAR

SELF-AWARENESS   UNDERSTANDING
SELF-REGULATION   ADAPTABILITY/
                          FLEXIBILITY

DECISIONS CHARACTERIZED BY

CONFIDENCE   COURAGE   INSIGHT   RESILIENCE   WISDOM

ORGANIZATIONAL OUTCOMES

ENHANCED DECISION
QUALITY

IMPROVED
PRODUCTIVITY

MORE CREATIVE
DECISIONS

REDUCED
ABSENTEEISM, ATTRITION,
LITIGATION, STRIFE

STRONGER
COLLABORATION

STRONGER
RELATIONSHIPS

SNAP BC begins with "See it," which uses mindfulness to begin the process of better managing ourselves in conflict. Many people are discovering the power of mindfulness as a means to be more productive and focused in getting work done successfully. However, mindfulness has benefits beyond productivity and focus. Through mindfulness, we can improve the quality of our interactions with our coworkers, increase present-moment awareness, and reduce stress.

Mindfulness might strike you as the latest buzzword in business and just another way of saying to "pay attention." But it means more than paying attention. It means being aware of our experiences, observing them without judgment, and responding to internal or external events from a place of compassion and clarity, rather than living unconsciously. Mindfulness practices give us the opportunity to gain insight into our behaviors, negative patterns, and habitual ways of responding and then consciously make choices for change. In the workplace, mindfulness can help managers be more effective, build better teams, make fewer rash decisions that could damage their or their company's reputation, and create strategies that can prevent conflict. As a result, managers and employees who practice mindfulness create a more positive work environment.

> *Mindfulness practices give us the opportunity to gain insight into our behaviors, negative patterns, and habitual ways of responding and then consciously make choices for change.*

All those years ago, when I was wrongly accused of sexual harassment and was hostage to anger and righteous indignation, I would have benefited from even a little bit of emotional management. Being unable to help myself in the face of these strong emotions was a terrible feeling because, on reflection, I was able to see that my reactions and behavior were not serving my best interests. But during interviews, I didn't think about managing my emotions. Instead, I thought about how I was being wronged and what might happen to my reputation. It was as if I were in a nightmare that I could not awaken from or in a trance.

Years after that incident, when my meditation and yogic studies to become a certified yoga instructor took me to India, I learned that the first step to developing those necessary emotional management skills was waking up from that trance and paying attention to what is going on inside me and in my environment. It lays the foundation for confidence, resilience, and wisdom. So we start with mindfulness in the first chapter before going on to each of the steps of the SNAP BC method.

CHAPTER ONE

Mindfulness—A Better Approach to Managing the Self in Conflict

Not everything that is faced can be changed, but nothing can be changed until it is faced.

—JAMES BALDWIN, AUTHOR, POET, AND ACTIVIST

N o change can occur without insight into our present behaviors. And that is only part of the equation. Having gained that insight, we must conclude that our behavior no longer serves our best interests and that a change is necessary. Thus, for change to occur, we must become aware of what we are doing, perceive the catalyst giving rise to our behavior, and realize that our present behavior will not help produce the results we want.

How is greater insight possible when we live so much of our lives unconsciously, on automatic pilot?

Living on Autopilot Is Pervasive

Most people live on autopilot—that state in which we principally are not acting with conscious awareness. It is a state characterized by a high degree of habitual action.

How much of our lives do we spend on autopilot? Think about it. When we wake up in the morning, our minds immediately switch on to begin planning the day. In the bathroom while brushing our teeth, our minds are already working out a solution to some business problem or preparing our children's lunch. In the shower, we ruminate about yesterday's meetings, arrange grocery lists, and rehearse for future speeches.

Do we taste the mintiness of the toothpaste or notice how our mouth feels revived? Do we feel the water on our skin, the soft lather from the soap, or the shampoo's perfume as we massage it into our hair?

Taking that first sip of coffee, do we pause to notice its pleasingly bitter flavor and texture in our mouth, its warmth on our tongue? Going to the car to drive to work or walking to the subway station, did we notice the cloudless sky? The dew on the grass? The birdsong?

For most of us, the answer is probably not because so many of us spend too much time with our minds and bodies in different places, rather than the same place at the same time. Consequently, we live mindlessly and are not present in our lives. Instead, we have habituated our minds to spend time in the future or the past. This phenomenon is nothing new. Eastern traditions put the origins of the study of mindfulness at least twenty-five hundred years ago, and it likely finds its roots in an earlier history. Today, the worldwide interest in mindfulness is a testament to the fundamental challenge it addresses—pervasive mindlessness.

Mindlessness allows our minds to engage in mischief that harms others. Biases are allowed to bloom unchecked. Emotions run free without any control or regulation. Constant rumination produces stress and anxiety, shortening our life spans.

Mindlessness is not altogether our fault. Scientists have estimated that we are exposed to eleven million pieces of sensory information per second. That is to say, the brain is asked to process eleven million pieces of sensory data per second. Yet we are only consciously aware of processing forty pieces per second. That is much, much less than even 1 percent. Other researchers estimate that perhaps 80 percent of our thinking occurs outside of our conscious awareness. In either case, the percentage of information we are consciously aware of processing is a small number. Because of the many, many choices and decisions we have to make every day, conscious deliberation would be exhausting and potentially dangerous. Letting our unconscious minds do this work is necessary if we are to effectively operate in the world.

Yet we cannot deny the harmful effects that attend such high levels of mindlessness. In the context of conflict, this reveals itself in the way so many of us habitually avoid conflict altogether, usually because of fear. This is not helpful for conflict resolution. Another way is how we rely on snap judgments or stereotypes in dealing with those with whom we are in conflict. This dynamic can prevent us from seeing the other's basic humanity, causing us instead to act on the basis of stereotypes or prejudice.

So many of us habitually avoid conflict altogether, usually because of fear. This is not helpful for conflict resolution.

Having said that our brains seem to be set up for unconscious action does not mean we are helpless or that we shouldn't try to do something about it. We can strive to bring more deliberate attention—mindfulness—into our daily lives to weaken the harmful effects of acting mindlessly in conflict.

A Mindful Approach to Managing the Self During Conflict

Mindfulness helps generate insight into our current ways of behaving and the catalysts that elicit that behavior by bringing our attention to the present moment with deliberate intention. The practice of mindfulness is

- a state of mind, a skill, a way of being;

- a way of paying attention to what arises in one's inner and outer world; and

- paying attention in an open way without criticizing, editorializing, judging, shaming, or blaming.

Deliberately bringing our attention to the present moment increases the chances for deeper, richer insight. This self-discovery helps us approach conflict from an inside-out orientation. With a mindful approach, we are like detectives aiming a lens at our subject, which is ourselves, and doing so with curiosity and gentleness. We use questioning, curiosity, and a nonjudgmental attitude and withhold criticism to simply discover what is there.

In the context of conflict, mindfulness can be particularly helpful. Mindfulness can help us notice if conflict is building or arising. It helps us bring awareness to our internal narrative and the stories we tell ourselves about what is actually happening in the conflict. It can help us notice and identify our emotions in real time and better regulate them. Mindfulness can help us perceive how conflict is manifesting in our bodies and help us interpret what that means for how we react to, and how others might perceive our reactions to, conflict. This process of mindful self-inquiry helps us break the trance of unconsciousness so that we can be less reactive and more deliberately responsive to conflict.

When we engage in mindful self-inquiry, we are looking to see what is arising in our inner and outer domains, and we do so without pointing fingers, establishing blame, or determining the origins of the conflict. Rather, we aim to discover how we ourselves (not the other person) are showing up in conflict for the purpose of self-insight. With this new insight, we can then decide whether our actions are beneficial or harmful to conflict resolution. We investigate in three domains:

1. Thoughts

2. Feelings

3. Bodily sensations

We want to begin to understand intimately what our thinking is like, what feelings we experience, and how our body reacts when we are in conflict. These areas are usually tuned to autopilot, and in conflict, they are areas in which we are unconsciously reactive. Using mindfulness, we train a light on those areas of darkness to discover what is there. In doing so, we gain valuable insight into our current conflict management behaviors and can better decide where to focus efforts to change.

SNAP OUT OF IT
Stop avoiding and mindlessly reacting.
Start responding with wisdom and courage.

To reduce conflict:

» See it: conflict as it arises

» Name it: emotions, thoughts, sensations

» Accept it: whatever arises, without running away

» Pause it: stop your action momentarily

» Breathe: trigger the relaxation response

» Choose it: create a wiser course of action

The SNAP BC Approach

The SNAP BC Approach is a step-by-step process for helping us to snap out of our unconscious and reactionary ways of responding to conflict. It helps us build the capacity—that is, the mental and emotional muscles—for working with conflict with greater resilience, confidence, and wisdom.

SEE IT

Seeing It involves becoming aware of the external environment—that is, the storm clouds of a conflict as they begin to brew. It also involves becoming aware of your internal state, seeing the thoughts, emotions, and bodily responses that arise as conflict occurs. Both external and internal awareness, which are conditions for insight, are the necessary first steps to any development and change.

NAME IT

Naming It involves discovering the words to describe and define your thoughts, feelings (used synonymously with emotions), and bodily sensations. When strong emotions arise, as they typically do in conflict, naming our emotions helps us

- stay present;

- calm the emotions;

- resist the impulse for distraction or avoidance;

- identify patterns in our emotional response to conflict;

- activate the prefrontal cortex of our brains (associated with executive functioning); and

- reduce the fight-flight-freeze response.

Naming thoughts and feelings

- tames automatic emotional responses;

- interrupts mindlessness;

- reinforces mindfulness; and

- helps identify patterns.

ACCEPT IT

Accept It means that we accept whatever arises—the ugly thoughts, fear, or stress—without resisting it. In other words, we accept that these are our current circumstances and resist in engaging in wishful thinking, which can promote an unwillingness to deal with what is in front of us. Accepting what is does not mean we have to like it or approve of it. By learning to accept, we build the muscles of staying with and not running away from or avoiding difficulty. Staying with difficult situations builds courage and confidence.

PAUSE IT

Pause It means to stop your action momentarily. When we pause our actions, just for a moment, we reduce reactivity and our habitual way of responding when we are in conflict. When we pause, we interrupt our patterns and create the mental space to develop an appreciation for looking at things differently. Pausing gives us a better chance at considering options and choosing a wise response.

> *When we pause, we interrupt our patterns and create the mental space to develop an appreciation for looking at things differently. Pausing gives us a better chance at considering options and choosing a wise response.*

BREATHE

Breathing deeply is not just a cliché. Deep breathing activates the parasympathetic nervous system and the vagus nerve, which calms the body and triggers the relaxation response. This helps us better access higher-order brain functions, such as problem solving, creativity, flexible thinking, planning, and impulse control so that we can skillfully respond rather than unconsciously react. Breathing to trigger the relaxation response has mental and physical benefits beyond better cognition and impulse control.

Research shows that when people watch their breath, even for a little while, they sleep better at night, reduce stress, and increase energy.

Like pausing, breathing gives us a better chance to choose wisely. In fact, one of the simplest ways to recenter or ground yourself is to stop whatever you are doing and shift your attention to the physical sensation of taking a few deep breaths. Notice and watch your breath as you breathe in through your nostrils and exhale through your nostrils. Noticing your breath establishes you squarely in the present moment.

Seeing, naming, accepting, pausing, and breathing in preparation for, and during, conflict puts us in a better position to choose a response that is in accord with our values, noble intentions, and higher self.

CHOOSE IT

Often when we are in the throes of conflict, our field of vision becomes so narrow that we perceive few options, much less consider them. But make no mistake: we have choices about how we respond in the face of conflict. As Viktor Frankl said, "Everything can be taken from a man but one thing: the last of the human freedoms—to choose one's attitude in any given set of circumstances, to choose one's own way."[1] That is exactly what seeing, naming, accepting, pausing, and breathing helps accomplish. They give us space to access the wisdom that resides in each of us.

With that wisdom, we can better distinguish between beneficial and detrimental actions and be guided toward skillful actions that have a chance of producing positive results. Acting with wisdom creates the opportunity to gain others' respect, draw out their best behavior, and inspire them to follow our actions. In this way, authentic leadership is cultivated and modeled for others.

The Goal Is to Work with Conflict, Not Eliminate It

Mindfulness is not a silver bullet or panacea. It will not eliminate conflict, nor is that the aim of mindfulness or the SNAP BC approach. In fact, the wish to eliminate conflict altogether is misguided because not all conflicts are unbeneficial. Well-managed conflict can help organizations produce more innovative solutions, generate a stronger sense of belonging, and promote employee engagement.

The aim of mindfulness and the SNAP BC approach to conflict is to offer a new way of relating to conflict, a way that enables you to be in conflict with a greater sense of confidence, courage, and strength. The aim of mindfulness techniques described in this book, tailored to the workplace conflict environment, is to help you build stronger emotional muscles so that you can navigate conflict with a greater sense of calm, emotional balance, compassion, and wisdom.

CHAPTER TWO

See It—Awakening from the Trance

Knowing others is wisdom;
Knowing oneself is enlightenment.
Mastering others is strength;
Mastering oneself is power.

—TAO TE CHING

It was my first meditation retreat: ten days of silence, no communicating with anyone. Ten days with just me and my mind, nine or more hours a day of simply watching the way my mind worked. Watching my mind in this way was a surprising and even disturbing experience. I was shocked at how many of my thoughts had me at the center, like I was always playing the leading role in a play. Were other meditators secretly watching me during the walking meditation? Why couldn't I take a break when I wanted to, instead of breaks being dictated by someone else? Were other meditators going to get to lunch first and take the best pieces of fruit? Why couldn't meditators wash their clothes without making so much noise and disturbing me during my nap time? What a surprise it was to learn how much I prioritized concern for myself with comparatively little for others. This first retreat put me on a path to awakening, a journey of continuously throwing off the chains of unconscious habit and donning new attire that comes with an increasingly awakened mind. The insights I've attained from this path I share with you, that it may contribute to greater self-awareness and workplace peace.

On Autopilot in Conflict

Most of us are on autopilot in the ways we respond to conflict. Often our response does not reflect a deliberate, intentional mind-state, but rather a mindless, reactionary one. A team's failure to include you on an important distribution list might draw a withering email response.

Like the record triggered by a scratch, playing music in a loop over and over again, our triggers activate the behaviors that we repeat without thinking.

A respectful request to turn down your music in an open cubicle workspace might result in a sharply worded response, which you post on your social media account. Receiving a report riddled with errors might provoke a public upbraiding. A colleague who takes credit for your work might also receive a rebuke on social media. Such reactive behaviors may promote greater conflict, foster poor morale, or even result in disciplinary actions. At its worst, responding to conflict while on autopilot can result in employees getting even with each other, retaliatory behavior, and even physical assault. I've handled many cases in which managers, insulted by allegations made against them, retaliated by denying promotions or attractive job assignments. Thus, the consequences of responding to conflict with mindless, reactionary behavior can be severe.

The way we show up in conflict is often the result of habit. Whether we tend to engage with conflict, avoid it, accede to others' wishes, compete with others, compromise, or collaborate, our behavior reflects a habitual mindset adopted over time through repeated action. Like the record triggered by a scratch, playing music in a loop over and over again, our triggers activate the behaviors that we repeat without thinking.

Our automatic response—the music we play—is the outward behavior that others observe. However, if we view human experience as an iceberg, our observable, conscious behavior is the tip that lies above the waterline. Lying beneath and outside our conscious awareness is a vast area that reflects the many factors that influence the behavior others observe.

Factors that influence our behaviors in response to conflict, as well as behaviors in other areas of life, include our perceptions, attitudes, beliefs, and values. In turn, these are influenced by a host of messages we received about conflict from our parents, mentors, peers, religion, education, geography, and so on. Altogether, these form our views about conflict. For example, our attitude about how we should respond to conflict is shaped by what our parents told or modeled for us. Watching the way our parents handled conflict as we grew up, we might conclude that it is a singularly destructive force to avoid. Our religious training may have impressed upon us the desire to be accommodating. The cultural mores of our home country may have taught that one should compete to win in any conflict. Likewise, whether we believe conflict can play a valuable role in human interaction and growth is similarly influenced.

Although largely outside of our conscious awareness, these underlying perceptions, attitudes, beliefs, and values drive our habitual responses to conflict. In addition, our body's response to stress plays a role. When the stress of conflict activates our fight-flight-freeze response, the stage is set for our emotions to overwhelm and undermine our higher-order thinking. We relate to employees with whom we are in conflict more from a stance of these habit patterns rather than a conscious, deliberate intention.

By awakening, we can bring these influences into conscious awareness. When we See It—that is, when we see what drives our behavior—we take a giant step toward reducing habit's hold on us.

As we awaken, we are better able to see the underlying beliefs, attitudes, and so on and begin to disrupt or loosen their hold on us. We take the first step toward freeing ourselves from the chains of our habit-driven minds. By using mindfulness tools, we are able to retrain our minds to observe the action as distinct from the layers of story-telling and judgment we add on top. By waking up to what's really happening, we begin the journey of acting with intention, delibera-tion, and consciousness.

Awakening allows us to begin to discover our unconsciously held views about conflict. Do we believe we must win this conflict at all costs? Do we value doing anything to keep the peace? Is our attitude "Never let them see you sweat?"

Awakening allows us to recognize the stories we tell ourselves about those with whom we are in conflict: that they're ungrateful, selfish, clueless, arrogant. And it allows us to recognize the stories and judgments we make about ourselves: I'm never any good at handling conflict; this is such a waste of time; nobody cares what I want; addressing this will only make matters worse. In recognizing our thoughts about conflict, ourselves, and others, we can begin to question their usefulness, and if we decide that they no longer serve us, to disrupt and redirect them.

Awakening helps us get in touch with our body's responses and the information that it conveys to us, furthering our understanding about how we show up in conflict. We can notice our jaws clench, stomachs tighten, perspiration increase. Doing so helps to inform us about what is happening or what we think is about to happen. By becoming more mindful of our bodies' signals, we are better positioned to regulate our emotions and calm ourselves down.

Being More Present Leads to Greater Connection with Others

Turning off autopilot and being more awake and fully present helps us to better see how things really exist in the world right now. This is valuable for the workplace because it allows us to connect with peers, direct reports, and bosses from a place of greater presence, genuineness, curiosity, and concern rather than superficiality and habit. Have you noticed the change in an employee's demeanor, the joy that spreads across their face when you praise them for a job well done? What does it feel like in your body when you as a manager criticize an employee's poor performance? How does the employee's appearance change when receiving this news? What goes through your mind when your decisions are overruled by your bosses? What happens in your body when you witness a colleague's mistreatment?

I am conventionally labeled an African American woman. Some of my colleagues, who are conventionally labeled white American liberals, would say that they cannot know what it is like to live as a Black woman. I'm still not altogether sure about the underlying point they are trying to make. But any one of us can make the same statement about any one of us living on this planet, for none of us has had precisely the same experience, even if we are members of the same social groups.

I think this misses the point. If we are trying to better connect with, understand, and generate compassion for another human being, we don't need to duplicate their experience. Rather, if we slow down, pay attention, and are more present, we can all see the powerfully universal experiences that come from being human. Every human being is likely to experience emotions such as joy or anger at some point in their lives. Every human being is likely to feel they have been wronged, whether a little or egregiously, at some point in their lives.

When we are more awake and present, we are more attuned to ourselves and to others. Thus, the benefit of awakening extends beyond managing the self with greater skill in conflict and extends to the whole of one's work life, as well as one's personal life. If you are a manager and are genuinely present for your staff, you foster human understanding and connection. You enable workers to reconnect with our fundamental human needs and desires, allow us to be vulnerable and present with others' humanness, and promote the strengthening of the muscles for resilient presence. Workers become more engaged and productive in the organization. They want to work for you, and their morale improves. Workplaces are then happier places to work.

HOW ATTENTIVE ARE LEADERS?

According to Harvard Business School and the Potential Project:

» 47 percent of leaders' average time spent mind wandering, off task

» 70 percent of leaders report regularly being unable to be attentive in meetings

» 75 percent of leaders feel unmindful most of the time due to distractions and interruptions

---

Awakening and the SNAP BC approach

Without going out-of-doors, one can know
all he needs to know.
Without even looking out of his window,
one can grasp the nature of everything.
Without going beyond his own nature,
one can achieve ultimate wisdom.
Therefore the intelligent man knows all he
needs to know without going away,
And he sees all he needs to see without looking elsewhere,
And does all he needs to do without undue exertion.

—TAO TE CHING, TRANSLATED BY ARCHIE J. BAHM

The SNAP BC method begins with See It because awareness (seeing) is the first step in the process of awakening to what is happening when we're in conflict. When we spend time in the past or future, we lose our ability to be present with and attend to what is happening in front of us and within us, right here and now.

> *When we spend time in the past or future, we lose our ability to be present with and attend to what is happening in front of us and within us, right here and now.*

Gaining insight into the way things exist now is critical if we are to change behavior that no longer serves us. If an unconscious conflict management style doesn't serve our needs and we want to change, the first step is to bring the unconscious style into conscious awareness. If we are in the dark about what we are doing, we need to shine a light so we can see it and better deal with it. Trying to change our behavior without first developing some insight into it is like driving down a dark country road without headlights on.

Mindfulness is the tool we use to begin the process of waking up from our habitual mindset of being on autopilot.

The first step is to relearn how to pay attention and be more fully present to what is happening within and outside us right here, right now. A mindful approach to self-discovery helps us approach the task of uncovering the unconscious from the inside out. It is a process of inquiry that increases the chances for deeper, richer insight into the self. The subject of mindful inquiry is ourselves. We are detectives and use curiosity, gentle questioning, and the withholding of judgment and criticism to simply discover what is there. This mindful approach to inquiry seeks not to point fingers, establish blame, or even determine the origins of a conflict. Rather, we aim to discover how we—not the other people—show up in conflict.

We inquire into three domains: our thoughts, feelings, and bodily sensations. We want to begin to understand intimately what our thinking is like, what feelings we experience, and how our body reacts when we are in conflict. It is in these three areas that we are unconsciously reactive when we are operating on autopilot.

This process of waking up allows us to begin to shift from subjective overidentification with the self to a more objective viewpoint. As Eckhart Tolle says, it helps to be aware of what our minds are doing without being totally trapped by what our minds are doing.

The deep understanding we get from the gentle, nonjudging inquiry of mindfulness has some stickiness and begins to shape how we show up in conflict situations. What we come to understand stays with us because there is no separation between the learner, what is learned, and the process of learning. By learning how to be aware of our reactions in the moment and giving space to—by not judging— what arises, we develop deep awareness and understanding, and such learning is likely to stay with us.

How Mindful in Conflict Are You?

How aware are you of what's going on in your inner and outer environments during conflict? The Mindful Management of Self in Conflict (MMSC) Scale helps you assess how tuned in you are to how you show up in conflict now. With insight from scores, you will be able to leverage strengths, develop capacity in weak areas, and better target developmental resources for cultivating emotional resilience and conflict competence.

The scale consists of statements about what you may experience when in conflict with someone. Using a 1 to 5 scale, where 1 means "strongly disagree" and 5 means "strongly agree," indicate to what degree you agree or disagree with each of the following statements. When evaluating the statements, it may be helpful to recall a specific instance of conflict with someone and how you responded. Please answer according to what really reflects your experience rather than what you think your experience should be, and treat each item separately from every other item.

Mindful Management of Self in Conflict Scale[1]

1 Strongly Agree	2 Agree	3 Neither Agree or Disagree	4 Disagree	5 Strongly Disagree

	1	2	3	4	5
I could be experiencing some feeling or emotion and not be conscious of it until sometime later.	O	O	O	O	O
I criticize myself for the thoughts I'm thinking.	O	O	O	O	O
I can communicate an idea in many different ways.	O	O	O	O	O
When I experience uncomfortable bodily sensations, I feel calm soon after conflict is over.	O	O	O	O	O
I judge uncomfortable bodily sensations as bad or inappropriate.	O	O	O	O	O

	1	2	3	4	5
I am willing to work at creative solutions to the problem.	○	○	○	○	○
I notice sensations happening in my body.	○	○	○	○	○
I experience uncomfortable sensations in my body.	○	○	○	○	○
I pause without immediately reacting.	○	○	○	○	○
I am willing to listen and consider alternatives for handling a problem.	○	○	○	○	○
I notice distressing thoughts or images I am having.	○	○	○	○	○
I criticize myself for having inappropriate emotions.	○	○	○	○	○
I have the self-confidence necessary to try different ways of behaving.	○	○	○	○	○
I criticize myself for the feelings I'm having.	○	○	○	○	○
I am able to have distressing thoughts or images without getting taken over by them.	○	○	○	○	○
It seems I am "running on automatic" without much awareness of what I'm doing.	○	○	○	○	○

TOTAL: _____

INTERPRETATION OF RESULTS

The scale assesses self-knowledge in four domains that are relevant to mindfulness in the context of interpersonal conflict as it is happening or as it develops: awareness, acceptance, self-regulation, and cognitive flexibility. Because the MMSC Scale works at the intersection of mindfulness (awareness/attention) and conflict, it is well suited for those in a workplace environment who are interested in improved conflict management, emphasizing an inside-out approach. Thus, the scale is useful for

- individuals who want to increase their own conflict competence, such as leaders,

- supervisors, managers, team leads; and

- those supporting such efforts, such as alternative dispute resolution practitioners, human resources managers, labor and employment professionals, mediators, consultants, and coaches.

There is no threshold or cut-off score for interpreting your responses. Further, these scores may change over time as your experience and skillfulness change, so please bear this in mind as you read your results.

AWARENESS

The ability to observe or act with cognizance of present-moment experience are each an element of mindful awareness. To assess your self-knowledge about awareness, calculate the sum of items 1, 7, 11, and 16. Higher scores suggest higher levels of observation or acting with awareness of present-moment events when in conflict. Possessing and behaving with present-moment awareness of one's internal and external environment is foundational to improved conflict management.

ACCEPTANCE

The ability to allow unwanted experiences to occur without judging, struggling against, or resisting them is a hallmark of acceptance. To assess your self-knowledge about acceptance, compute the sum of items 2, 5, 12, and 14. **Lower** scores reflect greater ability to allow unwanted experiences to occur without judging, struggling against, or resisting them. Greater levels of acceptance are associated with increased attention, openness, and cognitive flexibility in decision making.

SELF-REGULATION

The ability to modulate physiological responses to emotions to promote more internally beneficial and socially acceptable responses is the key feature of self-regulation. To assess your self-regulation ability, compute the sum of items 4, 8, 9, and 15. Higher scores suggest greater ability to modulate physiological responses to emotions and stay calm in conflict situations.

COGNITIVE FLEXIBILITY

Cognitive flexibility relates to a person's awareness of communication alternatives, willingness to adapt to the situation, and self-efficacy in being flexible.[2] To assess your cognitive flexibility, compute the sum of items 3, 6, 10, and 13. Higher scores suggest greater cognitive adaptability and agility in conflict situations. Greater cognitive flexibility is associated with creativity and enhanced decision making.

Scores in the higher range (although lower for the acceptance items) indicate that you are more able to bring mindful awareness to these domains in conflict situations. Even so, this book will help you deepen your capacity to bring mindful awareness to and manage the thoughts, emotions, and bodily sensations that arise, particularly in conflict situations.

Lower scores (although higher for the acceptance items) indicate increased opportunity to turn off autopilot and build capacity for mindful awareness. The good news is that this is an excellent time to access the existing tools and wisdom that help develop stronger mindfulness muscles. Tools to increase basic awareness and to train the mind to be more fully present and aware include online or in-person programs, corporate programs, books like this one, and mindfulness meditation apps and groups.

Developing the Ability to Awaken with Mindfulness

Suppose we recognize and accept that it would be beneficial to awaken from our trance of mindlessly reacting to conflict, see how we respond to conflict in the moment, and, if we choose to, practice a wiser strategy. How do we begin to wake up to the way we relate to conflict and being in conflict? Where do we begin?

We begin with exercises that help us rebuild the capacity and strengthen our muscles for awareness. When we spend unhealthy amounts of time ruminating about the past or planning for the future, we are strengthening our muscles for distraction and weakening our muscles for mindful presence. Mindfulness exercises counteract that tendency.

WHAT IS MINDFULNESS ANYWAY?

Mindfulness is a way of paying attention to what arises in one's inner and outer world. It is a state of mind and paying attention in an open way without criticizing, editorializing, judging, shaming, or blaming ourselves or the phenomenon that arises. Mindfulness training helps cultivate that state of mind by using techniques that help increase self-awareness and help persons self-regulate thoughts, emotions, and behaviors.

Mindfulness, which has roots in Eastern spiritual traditions, is and has been practiced for more than two millennia by people all over the world of many faiths or no faith. You can have faith in a Creator, or Higher Power, or none at all and practice mindfulness without any conflict or incompatibility.

At the beginning of the chapter, I shared my experiences while at a silent meditation retreat. I enjoy participating in retreats because they help me deepen my practice. This also enables me to more skillfully engage in the work that I do.

You don't need to participate in silent meditation retreats to experience the benefits of mindfulness. The idea that mindfulness and meditation take hours of effort is just one misunderstanding that people have. The box describes others.

MISUNDERSTANDING MINDFULNESS

I can't meditate because my mind never becomes quiet, no matter how hard I try.

When you sit to practice meditation, you may notice that your mind is a busy place—everyone's mind is busy. Traditional Buddhist meditation teachers call this "monkey mind." It can be uncomfortable at first to notice how active the mind is when previously you were not aware of this phenomenon, although it was happening all the same. It is not possible to stop thoughts from arising. Thinking is a central feature of our minds. But as the Dalai Lama says, we have the power to let each thought go, and we can train our minds to do so. When you train to let thoughts go, you may begin to notice the gap between each one. Meditation trains our minds so that we can expand the gaps between thoughts and cultivate a certain quiet or peace in that space.

Getting benefits from meditation takes years of practice.

In the late 1970s, renowned teacher Jon Kabat-Zinn developed an eight-week mindfulness-based stress-reduction program that helped people cope with chronic disease, depression, stress, and anxiety. After just two months, people experienced greater feelings of calm, less pain, and less stress, among other benefits. In fact, you can experience many of these benefits immediately following your first practice session. Many of the people I work with, including workplace professionals, report feeling more calm, less anxious, and less stressed after a few short sessions.

I would have to put in too much time every day to benefit from meditation.

Many people think that meditation requires finding a quiet space and sitting on a special cushion in a special posture for a long period of time. This is one meditation technique, but it's not the only one. Many teachers recommend meditating for twenty minutes every day, but even five to ten minutes of meditation a day can make a difference. Mindfulness meditation is very flexible. You can bring mindful awareness to any activity: walking to the car, making a cup of tea, or brushing your teeth. Mindfulness is more than a formal activity that we do only for certain periods of time, while the rest of the time, we just let it go and slip back into our unconscious, reactive way of being.

I have to practice Buddhism or some other religion to meditate.

You don't need to belong to a specific religion or have specific spiritual beliefs to meditate. Meditation is a practice for training the mind. Although most religions have meditative practices, you don't need to hold spiritual or religious beliefs to practice meditation. Because mindfulness and other practices are about training the mind, meditation is not in conflict with any religion, philosophy, agnosticism, or atheism. People meditate to gain wisdom about their interior landscape, experience inner quiet, and improve their mental and physical health.

# *A Basic Mindful Awareness Exercise*

Before you practice the exercise, read the entire section.

WHAT YOU'LL NEED

- Ten minutes when you are not too tired, sleepy, or distracted by life events to concentrate

- A relatively quiet space

- A timer

- A comfortable chair or cushion to sit on

THE POSTURE

On a chair or a cushion on the floor, sit in a position so that your body is grounded, balanced, comfortable, and alert. Imagine yourself as a king or queen on the throne preparing to receive subjects. If sitting on a chair, put your feet flat on the floor or some other stable object. If sitting on a cushion, cross your legs. Let the buttocks be balanced and firmly connected with whatever is underneath them. Lift the spine up all the way through the crown of the head, as if a string connected your parts from the sitting bones all the way up the spine to the top of the head. Dip the chin slightly toward the chest, as if holding an orange. Let the shoulders and arms be loose and relaxed. Place your hands on your thighs or lap.

INTENTION AND AIM: NO GOALS

As with other forms of contemplative practice, such as yoga, it is helpful to set an intention for the mindfulness session. When we set an intention, we are preparing to move our minds in a certain direction. We are saying to ourselves, "I'm about to undertake a task with deliberateness and intentionality." We are urging our minds to be better prepared to stay present with the contemplative activity. When setting an intention, we are not trying to achieve some goal in the activity. For example, with mindfulness meditation, we are not trying to completely clear our minds of all thoughts. We are not trying to achieve a state of utter peace. Nor are we trying to take a mental trip to some other, better place, however we define it.

Rather, the aim of our mindfulness practice is to try to pay attention to what is happening inside of us as it happens and to do so in a nonjudging, compassionate way. So when we set an intention, it should be aligned with these aims. One intention you may want to try out is "With kindness toward myself, I sit to train and develop my mind so that I may be of greater benefit to myself and others." You should feel free to create your own intention, one that is wholesome, aligned with the aims of the practice, and not overly ambitious. Then start the timer.

THE BASIC PRACTICE

To begin, allow your body to feel relaxed. Try to generate a sense of openness or open awareness and receptivity, as if you were in the presence of a trusted teacher or loving friend.

Though your body is relaxed and open, let your mind be alert and curious, as though you were reading a page-turner of a book.

Breathe.

Turn your attention to your breathing. Focus on the place in your body where you most readily and deeply connect to your breath. For most people, this is the belly or chest. Let your breath be your anchor for this exercise.

As you breathe in, notice how the belly or chest rises as the breath moves into your body. As you breathe out, notice how the belly or chest falls as the breath leaves your body. Follow the entire breathing cycle. As you breathe in, notice the pause at the top of the breath. As you breathe out, notice the pause at the bottom of the breath. Don't try to manipulate the breath in any way, such as by consciously slowing it down or holding or retaining it. Simply observe the breath, and try to do so with gentleness and open awareness. Simply observe as you breathe in and out.

Distractions will arise. A distraction is anything that takes your attention away from your anchor—your breath. You may have a thought, hear a sound, feel some emotion, or feel something happening in your body. This is normal. We cannot stop our thoughts or any of these things from happening. Our task is to try to be aware that distractions are occurring and to do so without judging or criticizing what is arising. We try to notice when we are thinking, for example, without getting entangled in the thought or story. To do this, we can say silently and gently, "Thinking"; try to let the thought flow by, like a cloud against the sky; and then return awareness to the breath.

So the exercise consists of placing our awareness on an object—our breath—trying to notice when our mind moves from that object because of distractions, and bringing our attention back to that object. We continue in this fashion until the timer sounds. If you are new to this practice, I recommend five minutes to start. If you are more experienced, set the timer to a time where you can sit comfortably without undue agitation.

When the timer sounds, slowly release your awareness of the breath. As you continue to breathe, let yourself become aware of your body on the chair or cushion and your presence in the environment. You can take a few deep inhalations and exhalations to encourage this return.

Now that you have read all of the instructions and have gathered what you need, you are ready to begin.

REFLECTION QUESTIONS

If you like, write responses to the following questions on the lines that follow each.

How did you find this exercise?

_____

_____

_____

_____

What was the experience of sitting still and simply watching the rise and fall, coming and going of the breath, like for you?

_____

_____

_____

_____

What did you learn, discover, or notice about your ability to pay sustained attention to a particular object—your breath?

_____

_____

_____

_____

What did you notice or learn about distractions, such as thoughts, emotions, or sounds as they occurred?

_____

_____

_____

_____

Did you become entangled in the distractions, or were you able to watch them with some level of objectivity and let them go?

_____

_____

_____

_____

What would support you in incorporating such a practice regularly in your life?

_____

_____

_____

_____

What likely obstacles would you need to address?

_____

_____

_____

_____

Mindfulness in Conflict Visualization

This mindfulness visualization begins the process of seeing how we show up in conflict. Before you begin the exercise, read the entire section.

WHAT YOU'LL NEED

- Ten minutes when you are not too tired, sleepy, or distracted by life events to concentrate

- A relatively quiet space

- A timer

- A comfortable chair or cushion to sit on

THE EXERCISE

The aim of this exercise is to maintain awareness on an object: the remembered conflict. During the exercise, you will recall the conflict in as much detail as possible—where you were, what you and others were saying and doing, and what you were thinking and feeling. Visualizing in this amount of detail can be difficult the first time you try it because your mental muscles are not well trained. Try not to judge any difficulty or worry about it. You may also find that distracting thoughts arise. That's normal. Try to be aware that a distraction occurred, and then simply bring your mind back to the remembered conflict. Again, try not to judge the distractions, get entangled in them, or worry about them. Over time as you practice, you may become more adept at noticing and handling distractions. They may even occur with less frequency.

Choose a conflict to work with. It's best to start with something simple, the same as you would work with the lightest weights at the gym if you were a beginner or had not been there for a long time. If you started with the heaviest weights, you would risk injury, discouragement, or demotivation. Similarly, avoid choosing a situation that is too overwhelming. Instead, choose a conflict that has caused you some suffering but does not inspire self-criticism, trigger self-judgment, or pose an existential threat.

THE POSTURE AND INTENTION

On a chair or a cushion on the floor, sit in a position so that your body is comfortable—not too stiff and not too loose. Set an intention for the session, for example, "With kindness toward myself, I am sitting to gain insight into my way of being during conflict so that I may be of greater benefit to myself and others." Then start the timer.

THE PRACTICE

To begin, allow your body to feel relaxed. Try to generate a sense of openness, open awareness, and receptivity, as if you were in the presence of a loving pet or trusted friend.

Let your mind be alert and curious, as though you were interested in seeing what your pet was going to do next or hearing your friend describe a trip to an exotic location. Have an intention to be present for and curious about what arises next.

Breathe.

Turn your attention to your breathing. Focus on the place in your body that you most readily and deeply connect to your breath. For most people, this is the belly, chest, or nostrils. Let your breath be your anchor. You can always return to the breath moving in and out of your body if you want to leave the visualization.

As you breathe in, attend to the feeling. Notice that you are breathing in. As you breathe out, attend to the feeling. Notice that you are breathing out. Follow the entire breathing cycle. As you breathe in, notice the pause at the top of the breath. As you breathe out, notice the pause at the bottom of the breath. Observe the breath with gentleness, presence, and open awareness, without judging or criticizing what is arising. Simply observe as you breathe in and out.

Continue following your breath until you get some sense of balance and stability, even if it is slight, fleeting, or temporary. This might take a few minutes.

Next, visualize a time when you were in conflict with someone at work. Choose a conflict of light intensity and scope. If you cannot identify a light work-related conflict, choose one from other areas of your life. To keep the intensity and scope light, avoid choosing a conflict with a parent or spouse.

Gently turn your awareness away from your breath and to the remembered conflict. Try to generate specificity around the conflict. Where were you? Who else was involved? Then try to get a sense of the conflict unfolding and your experience in it as it did. What was happening? What did you say? What did others say? What were you thinking about the conflict, the others in it? What emotions did you experience? What was the body language like, your demeanor? Try to see yourself and others as clearly as possible in the conflict. Don't worry if the details are difficult to visualize. Even if you cannot see the event clearly, see if you can get a feeling for the tone of the experience, similar to how you feel when you awaken from a vivid dream.

As you do this exercise, try to refrain from judging or criticizing your experience. Like you would with a dear friend in distress, just be with yourself with care and compassion. If judgments or criticism arise, just note that you are thinking, and return to your breath and memory.

Continue remembering the conflict, along with its details, until the timer sounds. Just try to watch and be with it as the drama unfolds, with yourself as one of the main players.

When the timer sounds, slowly release your awareness of the conflict, and gently turn your attention back to your breath and the present moment. Continue following your breath, and let yourself become aware of your surroundings. You can inhale deeply and exhale deeply to help return your awareness to the present.

Without entanglement or fanfare, allow yourself to feel a sense of accomplishment, much as you would for successfully undertaking a challenge.

Now that you have read all of the instructions and have gathered what you need, you are ready to begin.

REFLECTION QUESTIONS

If you like, write responses to the following questions on the lines that follow each.

How did you feel about this exercise?

_____

_____

_____

_____

What was the experience of sitting still and simply replaying the conflict in your mind like for you?

_____

_____

_____

_____

Did you discover anything about how you showed up in the conflict you visualized?

_____

_____

_____

_____

How easy or difficult was it to refrain from judging or criticizing thoughts as you let the conflict unfold in your mind?

_____

_____

_____

_____

What did you learn, discover, or notice about the conflict itself?

_____

_____

_____

_____

Seeing It in Context and Preparing to Name It

Just like you can be aware of what your mind is doing without being defined by it, you can be aware of how your emotions come and go without being trapped by them. As you reflect on the exercises, you may realize that your thoughts and emotions come and go on their own. It might seem as if you don't control them.

When you were engaged in the basic mindfulness exercise, you might have noticed one or more emotions rising to the surface and then moving on. Distracting thoughts might have entered your awareness, and you might have noticed how difficult it is to let them come and go. The mind, by nature, is a busy place. Tolle and others call this busyness "self-talk" and suggest that we don't have to identify with it.

The practice of mindfulness and the process of waking up means that we can begin to shift our perspective from an immersed sense of me, my, and I, to a more objective and expansive sense of what is going on in and around us. We are not our thoughts or emotions. For example, when we live mindfully, we see thoughts or emotions arising, observe them, and let them go.

The thinking mind is inherently subjective. Practicing mindfulness helps us take a step back and see the mind and the way it functions objectively. This is a process of uncovering and discovery that shifts thoughts and emotions from unseen and unconscious to seen and conscious. This capacity to observe thoughts and emotions arising without being trapped by them enables us to gain insight. Instead of being unconsciously driven so that we react to events, we can begin to take more meaningful action.

The process of waking up can be enlivening, scary, intriguing, maddening, disappointing, revealing, disheartening, disturbing, mind-blowing, and more. It is a practice that takes courage. Initially, when we stop, turn off autopilot, and turn on manual controls, the results for how we approach conflict can be unpredictable.

CHAPTER THREE

Name It—How to Tame What Arises

An emotion, which is a passion, ceases to be a passion,
as soon as we form a clear and distinct idea thereof.

—BARUCH SPINOZA, *ETHICS*

When I attended law school, I did not adapt very well to the high-stress environment. So I sought help from student counseling services. Along with using other therapeutic techniques, the counselor outfitted me with a wearable biofeedback device. The device consisted of a clip with sensors that measured the amount of perspiration on my skin—increased perspiration is theoretically an indicator of stress—and a small box clipped to a belt. I wore the clip on my index finger, wires sent data to the box, and the box signaled me when my stress level increased.

Although the biofeedback helped me become aware of stress and make appropriate changes, wearing the device was pretty embarrassing.

My stress level spiked during a particular class. I had a vague notion the class was distasteful but had no idea it was as bad as my little biofeedback device indicated.

Today I think if that counselor had taught me how to pay attention to what was going on inside me, I would have realized much sooner how stressful that class was. Looking back, I remember that every time I entered that professor's class, I was breathless, angry, and fearful. I remember thinking things like, "What a jerk. I can't believe I have to endure this nonsense."

Applying the mindfulness technique of naming would have shifted what I was feeling and thinking from amorphous to concrete. I would have learned and practiced a skill that enabled me to reduce my anxiety then and throughout my life. And I wouldn't have had to wear that embarrassing device.

The Difficulty of Staying Focused

In Chapter 2, "See It," we started practicing a general mindfulness exercise to increase our awareness in general and learn how to stay more present. Then, we practiced awareness concerning a specific conflict. The practice involved becoming aware of how that conflict arose and unfolded, our thoughts about it and those involved in it, the emotions we experienced, and how our bodies responded to the conflict.

These practices began to retrain your attention muscles, to strengthen your ability to be more present, and to help you stay focused on a particular subject (in this case conflict) so that you could see what was happening. The goal of that exercise is to provide you with information about how you show up in conflict. This method of developing self-insight happens from the inside out. With insight, you can better discern what behaviors are beneficial and what are not. In this way, you can decide how to correct the latter.

Keeping our attention on a subject so that we can examine what's there is an important element in developing self-insight. But it can be difficult to stay focused. During the conflict visualization exercise, you might have noticed that difficulty. You might have been surprised at the number of distracting thoughts you had. Do you recall what occurred in your mind during the visualization? Maybe you thought, "This chair isn't as comfortable as I thought it would be," or "I'm thirsty," or "Has it been five minutes yet?" Maybe you thought all of these, or maybe one of a million other thoughts occurred to you.

The Wandering Mind

Often, thoughts pop into our minds unbidden, and they may not always be welcome. Some estimates put time spent in off-task thinking as high as 46.9 percent.[1] Our minds are wandering off task almost half the time. Neuroscientists are not sure why our minds wander and have such difficulty staying on task.

Several brain systems, collectively called the default network, appear to be involved in distracted, wandering, undirected thinking.[2] Surprisingly, executive function and memory systems, along with the default network, are also active during wandering thought. We usually think of executive function and memory systems as active when we are purposely engaged in remembering past events or imagining upcoming events. So when our minds are wandering, systems all across the brain are active. As Alva Noë, philosopher at the University of California, Berkeley, puts it, "Even spontaneous free thoughts arise out of memory and experience, it would seem. We are still very much engaged with the world, coupled to it, even when we are simply letting our minds wander."[3]

Interestingly, some data also suggest that what people are doing has only a small impact on whether their minds wander. Whether a person is watching television or writing a report doesn't seem to make much difference. And whether our minds wander off to a pleasant or unpleasant topic has little to do with the nature of our activities.[4]

> *A distracted mind usually means ruminating about the past or planning for the future, and both contribute to unhappiness in the present moment. As Harvard psychologists Matthew Killingsworth and Daniel Gilbert put it, "A wandering mind is an unhappy mind."*

Regardless of what we are doing, when our minds wander, we are less happy.[5] Thus, research about wandering minds supports the theoretical underpinnings of mindfulness and what I've heard from clients: a distracted mind usually means ruminating about the past or planning for the future, and both contribute to unhappiness in the present moment. As Harvard psychologists Matthew Killingsworth and Daniel Gilbert put it, "A wandering mind is an unhappy mind."

Moving from Wandering to Focused

It can be difficult to tame our mind and bring it under greater control, especially when we are beginning an intentional effort to do so. Our monkey mind may initially resist efforts to tame it, and it may find the swing from unchecked freedom to subjugation more than it can bear. A helpful approach is to use a middle way that gives the mind something to do while still nudging it toward present moment awareness.

Naming It (also called mental noting) is an effective way to direct the mind while furthering our awakening from the trance.

It might sound counterintuitive to say that giving the mind something concrete to do can coax it into being more in the present moment. Aren't we just giving the mind something else to ramble on about? On the contrary, by naming what is arising in the mind, we help to resettle the mind on the present.

The primary purpose of naming is to keep your mind present with whatever is arising and thereby reduce the trance we so often find ourselves in. Naming achieves this effect by helping us interrupt the mind's wandering and reestablish mindfulness. With our focus on the present, we have a better chance to deal skillfully with what is arising.

Naming has many other benefits. One is to help us increase our ability to recognize what is arising in the first place; that is, naming helps us see. Gil Fronsdal, a founding and guiding teacher of the Insight Meditation Center in California, who has a PhD in Buddhist studies from Stanford University and more than forty years practicing meditation, says, "The clearer one's recognition, the more effective one's mindfulness. Naming can strengthen recognition."[6]

Fronsdal continues, "Sometimes this can be a kind of truth-telling, when we are reluctant to admit something about ourselves or about what is happening." I have found that recognizing what is happening has a certain liberating effect. It's as if you've been troubled by a medical condition with a constellation of symptoms but no clear diagnosis. Once the doctor labels it—"No, not cancer, but irritable bowel syndrome"—our minds stop conjuring the worst, and we can relax in a type of assurance that comes from a concrete diagnosis, even if it is not innocuous. Similarly, when our minds are trapped in endless discursive-thinking loops or repeatedly emotional responses to the same stimulus, concretizing the thought or emotion can free us from the never-ending loop. Even if we might not like the diagnosis—rumination or jealousy, say—we derive a sense of satisfaction from having circumscribed the problem so that we now know better what we're dealing with.

Naming also helps us become aware of repetitive or habitual behaviors. When you see the vice president who screamed at you in the middle of the hallway or a quarrelsome colleague heading in your direction, does "I have to duck into a doorway" always arise in your mind? When another driver enters the highway without yielding, do you always become angry and think, "Don't they know what the yield sign means?" Identifying these patterns is an important part of the change process.

THE TECHNIQUE OF NAMING

In mindfulness meditation, naming is the technique of labeling a distracting event based on the six senses (we include thinking as a sense) that takes you away from your object of attention. To begin working with this practice, we name in simple terms, based on the sense that is activated. For example, if a sound takes us away from our object of attention, we name it "hearing." If we have an enticing thought that we want to pursue, we name it "thinking." Similarly, we name seeing, smelling, tasting, and feeling. When we are naming, we are not trying to tell a story about our experience. We are not trying to promote more discursive thinking and judgment. Because of this, the content of the distraction is unimportant. If the thought is brilliant or banal, if the smell is enticing or disgusting, if the emotion is warm or unwelcoming—all are treated as distractions from our aim of paying present-moment attention to our object of inquiry. We name the thing silently to ourselves, gently and without fanfare. Rather, like a chime that encourages us to come back to the present moment, we name something.

You can do naming, like any other mindfulness practice, almost anywhere and under most circumstances. Whatever the practice and wherever you do it, mindfulness reawakens us to the present.

For example, say you're in the park with your beloved black Labrador, Shelly. Suppose on this beautiful, sunny day, you're rubbing Shelly's tummy, being present with and attentive to your dog in an open and relaxed way. But what happens when distractions arise? Suppose an attractive person walks by. Or you hear sirens. Or you feel the rumble of the subway train as it speeds beneath you in the tunnel below the park. Any of these sensations might draw your attention away from your pet. By naming the sensation associated with what we are experiencing, we are able to redirect our attention to keep it focused on the task at hand. Naming builds the mental muscle of paying attention. Like athletes practicing their sport, your practice strengthens the skill of bringing attention back to the present moment.

At the park with your dog, Shelly, you name the sense involved in the distracting experience. So when the attractive person walks by, you would say, "Seeing." If you have some thoughts around seeing them ("I wish I could get their phone number"), you would name those thoughts "thinking." When the sound of sirens is the distraction, you would name it "hearing." When you feel the rumble of the subway train, you would name it "sensing" or "feeling." For how long do you carry on naming? Until you have sufficiently acknowledged what you are experiencing and the distraction subsides. As Gil Fronsdal puts it, you name until the thought "is no longer predominant."[7]

It is important to realize that you are not trying to name every single thing, only those that pull your attention away with some degree of persistence. Fleeting experiences that do not distract you in a sustained way require no naming. For example, as you pet Shelly, your stomach may growl because you didn't eat breakfast. If the growling is not persistent enough to distract you from Shelly and inspire you to go back home and whip up a four-course meal to satisfy your hunger, then naming is not required.

Preparing for Conflict

As is the case with "seeing" discussed in the last chapter, to effectively benefit from the naming strategy, you must practice the technique to develop some skillfulness. This is especially true in conflict situations because it may be difficult to even remember that you have the skills to draw on, let alone access them during such a state of high anxiety. Practice is everything.

The following sections provide a basic exercise for practicing naming, a deeper practice that uses naming to help identify habits or patterns, a naming exercise that includes a conflict visualization, and an immersive exercise that uses naming during mindfulness while walking.

A Mindfulness with Naming Exercise[8]

For this exercise, you will need a timer, chair or cushion, and relatively quiet space.

Read the instructions in their entirety before beginning the exercise.

After reading the instructions, sit in a comfortable position, and place your timer within arm's reach. And when ready, if you are new to mindfulness, set the timer for five minutes.

Set an intention for the mindfulness session that moves you in a positive direction. For example, "With kindness toward myself, I am sitting to gain insight into my way of being during conflict so that I may be of greater benefit to myself and others." Then start the timer.

Allow your body to relax. Try to generate a sense of open awareness and receptivity, as if you were in the presence of a loving pet or a trusted friend.

Let your mind be alert and curious, as though you were interested in seeing what your dog would do next or hearing your friend describe her trip to an exotic location. Generate an energetic intention that you will be present for whatever arises in the next five minutes.

Turn your attention to your breathing. Focus on the place in your body where you most readily and deeply connect to your breath. Let your breath be your anchor, the place you return to whenever your attention is drawn away.

As you breathe in, know that you are breathing in. As you breathe out, know that you are breathing out. Pay attention through-out the breathing cycle. As you breathe in, notice the pause at the top of the breath; as you breathe out, notice the pause at the bottom of the breath.

Observe your breath with a gentle, present, open awareness. Simply observe what arises without judging or criticizing. Like a curious baby exploring the world, generate a sense of nonjudging, open curiosity.

Thoughts, emotions, sounds, smells, sights, or bodily sensations will draw your attention away from your breath. This is normal. The key is to try to notice the moment when your attention is being drawn away. Often it can take several seconds or even minutes before we notice our focus is no longer on our object of attention. So it is a significant achievement when we are able to notice this pulling away of our attention.

When something draws your attention away, name the sensation, such as "thinking," "feeling," "hearing" "smelling," or "sensing" silently and softly, like a gentle nudge. Naming is not forceful or accusatory. Try not to get entangled in stories you might want to tell about what you're experiencing. Simply name the experience and then return your awareness back home, to your breath. Repeat this process every time your mind wanders from attention to your breathing.

Continue in this way until the timer sounds. Then, slowly release your focus on naming, and gently turn your attention back to your breath, back to the present moment, back to your surroundings. You can deeply inhale and exhale to encourage this return to the present.

Now, without entanglement or fanfare, allow yourself to feel a sense of accomplishment, much as you would for successfully undertaking some challenge.

 *REFLECTION QUESTIONS*

How did you find this exercise?

How easy or difficult was it to become aware that a distraction had occurred?

How did naming affect your experience with the distracting event?

Were you able to notice any storytelling that may have accompanied the naming?

How easy or difficult was it to refrain from judging, evaluating, or criticizing your experience?

_____

_____

_____

_____

NAMING OUR THOUGHTS

Another way to practice naming is to use the technique to notice habits or patterns, especially in one's thinking. By noticing the habitual ways in which our thinking minds relate to a subject, we can begin to see more clearly what modes of thinking are beneficial and to be maintained, and what are not and are to be abandoned. To determine what is beneficial and what is detrimental, ask yourself whether the thinking contributes to your happiness or unhappiness.

This exercise applies naming at a somewhat deeper level, still aiming to avoid entanglement in our stories and discursive thinking, while revealing the overall frame of our thinking.

The following is a nonexhaustive list of common ways we engage in thinking about a subject. Take a moment to familiarize yourself with these categories, and feel free to add to them. Then, when you're ready, try the basic naming exercise but with a focus on distracting thoughts. Try to notice when a distracting thought arises. When it does, name it "thinking," and add the appropriate categorical label. For example, you might say, "Thinking," and then add, "Analyzing." You can use this mindfulness technique throughout the day to help reestablish present moment awareness while noticing the types of trips your mind tends to take.

» **Remembering**

» **Reflecting**

» **Evaluating**

» **Judging**

» **Criticizing**

» **Analyzing**

» **Fantasizing**

» **Imagining**

» **Concocting**

» **Opining**

» **Ruminating**

What words would you add to this list?

Name It to Tame It

How do we know we're in conflict with someone? Most people do not take a deliberative process in which they methodically analyze what was said and done and assess how they feel about it. Rather, we know we are in conflict with someone because we experience a certain emotional feeling or charge. We are thrown off kilter, physically, mentally, and psychologically. Whether fear, anger, exasperation, or something else, we experience a change in our emotional state that signals something is awry and requires our attention. As Nisha Nair, University of Pittsburgh business professor puts it, we become "emotionally charged."

Yet likely no one taught you how to identify and manage your emotions, recognize them when they arise, and navigate your way through them. Most managers simply try their best to maneuver this terrain on their own, often with unsatisfactory results.

Even though leaders know their organizations pay a high price for unresolved workplace conflict, many still take the view that emotions—the very emotions that signal conflict—are destructive, distracting, scary, and to be avoided. Such a mindset is not helpful and is increasingly out of step with emerging views about constructive conflict resolution.

For centuries, the study of emotions was relegated to philosophers. But there has been a surge in research about emotions, how our understanding of them has changed over time, and their significance in our everyday lives. We are increasingly appreciating the profound role emotion plays in our culture, society, and workplace.

For example, the polling firm Gallup produces an annual *Global Emotions Report* to gauge the emotional and behavioral side of workers' lives. In the 2018 report, Americans indicated feeling stress, anger, and worry at the highest levels in a decade, making them among the most stressed people in the world.[9]

These emotionally charged individuals are the workers in your workplace. In Gallup's 2020 report taken during the scourge of the COVID-19 pandemic, they report a more complicated and somewhat contradictory picture. Remote workers reported generally better well-being while reporting higher levels of worry, sadness, loneliness, and anxiety than in-house workers. These differences may be attributed to how well-being is defined and its sensitivity to changing life experiences, and their emotional lives play a clear role in the conflict equation.

Leaders who promote organizational cultures that recognize and value the important role of emotional competency are rewarded with teams whose members are better at problem solving, innovation, and conflict management. For example, research indicates that teams can achieve higher performance if they have higher levels of emotional intelligence and are able to deal with their own emotions during problem-solving activities. Team members who are better able to deal with their own emotions may be more inclined to listen to alternative viewpoints and seek superior solutions without feeling threatened by the possibility of being wrong.[10]

In contemporary workplaces, conflicts with employees, like those who underperform, who subtly undermine colleagues, are toxic gossipers, and the like, are common, typically not addressed, and simmer beneath the surface, piling up over time until some last-straw event provokes a fiery managerial response. As long as leaders inadequately address workers' emotional selves, workplace conflict will act as a drag on performance, push morale and engagement downward, and increase litigation risk.

For organizational leaders who want to develop, model, and promote greater emotional competence among their workers, working with the mindfulness technique of naming can be particularly beneficial.

The key benefit of naming is that it develops emotional regulation skills. Neuroscience research using functional magnetic resonance imaging (fMRI) techniques shows that naming emotions—which psychologists call affect labeling—activates neural processes associated with carefully observing and perceiving the differences between one thing and another. Specialized analysis of fMRI data demonstrates connections between these analytical processes, emotional processes, and language processes. Psychologists with expertise in mindfulness are connecting these neuroscience studies with evidence from their research on emotions, expressive writing, and talk therapy techniques to suggest that naming engages emotional regulation and reduces processes involved in emotional reactions.[11] To put it simply, putting feelings into words can tone down emotional responses. Our ability to identify and call out humiliation, anger, or fear, for example, can help us tamp down emotional reactivity as well as calm down our bodies.

Emotion regulation is essential for adaptive behavior and mental health. Naming is particularly effective at calming strong emotions that occur in response to a threat because it activates processes that we use to think about emotions and process them.[12]

Emotion regulation is essential for adaptive behavior and mental health.

Dan Siegel, founder of the Mindsight Institute and UCLA clinical professor of psychiatry, puts it this way: "Name it to tame it." Siegel was speaking to parents about helping their children learn emotional regulation, but the idea speaks to adults as well.

Although the mindfulness practice of naming has been used for more than two millennia, the modern brain-imaging technique fMRI shows the neuroscience underpinning why it is effective.

Identifying Emotions versus Thoughts, Assessments, or Views

It can be difficult for us to have and use the vocabulary for emotions. We often express an evaluation, thought, view, or assessment about another person or situation rather than express how we were feeling (our emotions) behind it. For example, we might say that we feel it is unfair that we should have to deal with a conflict. Or that we feel like firing a troublesome employee. Yet these are not expressions of emotions or feelings but rather assessments or thoughts. As psychologist Marshall Rosenberg discusses in his popular book *Nonviolent Communication*, we often use words to describe what we think we are doing or what we think others around us are doing, rather than actually express what we really feel.[13]

One way to get at underlying emotions that accompany an event is to use the shortcut "I'm" along with an emotion. This is what Rosenberg advocates. For example, we can simply say, "I'm worried. I'm embarrassed. I'm afraid." We can immediately recognize and tune into the emotion. This stands in contrast to expressions such as "I feel that I shouldn't have to deal with this problem," or "I feel like I'm dealing with a bunch of children in this conflict," which describe what others are doing or are assessments. To practice identifying and naming emotions, start by using this structure "I'm … " along with a word or words from the feelings wheel in the sidebar box.

Feelings Wheel for Identifying and Naming Emotions

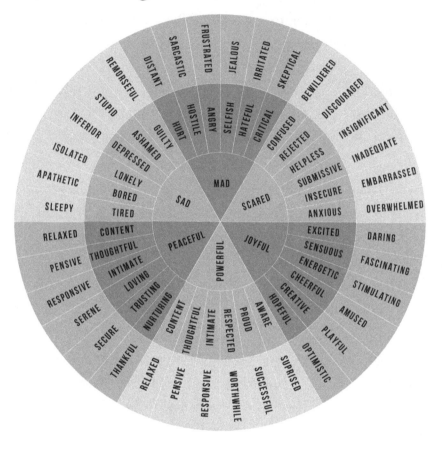

Source: Gloria Wilcox, "The Feeling Wheel: A Tool for Expanding Awareness of Emotions and Increasing Spontaneity and Intimacy," Transactional Analysis Journal 12, no. 4 (December 2017): 274-276, https://doi.org/10.1177/036215378201200411.

Naming Strong Emotions in a Conflict Visualization

In the preceding naming exercise, you may have been surprised to see how active the senses are and how easily they can capture our interest, taking our minds away from what we are doing. As you continue to work with these practices—what I call mental strength training—you will develop stronger mental muscles for paying attention to exactly what you want to, without the mind being so easily pulled away. Even after years of practice, as I have gained some facility at stilling the mind, I continue to marvel at how the still mind allows me to observe the never-ending, life-sustaining processes occurring in my body and mind—heart beating, mind thinking, pain coming and going, breath circulating, sounds rising and falling, and so much more. With so much happening with the senses, I find that focusing on one thing in my formal practice can help promote concentration and deepen insight. This is what we will do in this exercise.

Being emotionally charged is a strong indicator that conflict is afoot. And the inability to manage strong emotions, especially fear, is one of the principal responses that severely weakens our ability to be more skillful in conflict. For that reason, in this exercise we will work with naming strong emotions. By doing so, we will begin to awaken and familiarize ourselves with our emotional responses to conflict as well as build the skills to tame them.

To begin, prepare as you would in the Mindfulness with Naming exercise. Bring your awareness to the place in your body where you most readily and deeply connect to your breath. Continue in this way until you get a sense of stability, even if slight, fleeting, or temporary. This might take a few minutes.

Next, visualize a time when you were in conflict with someone at work. As before, choose a conflict of light intensity and scope. If you cannot identify a work-related conflict, choose one from another area of your life. Choose a conflict that has caused you some difficulty, but one that is not too overwhelming.

Gently turn your awareness away from your breath and to the remembered conflict. As before, try to generate as much specificity as you can around the conflict. Try to recall where the conflict arose. Without focusing on the "why," how did the conflict seem to arise? Who was involved? What happened? What did you say? What did others say? What was the body language like? Try to see yourself and others as clearly as possible in the conflict. Don't worry if the details are difficult to visualize. Even if you cannot see the event clearly, see if you can get a feeling for the tone of the experience, similar to how you feel when you awaken from a vivid dream.

Remembering the conflict and the feeling of what it was like being in it, see if you can name the strong emotions that you observed yourself feeling. As you vividly remember the conflict, what emotions are arising: fear, anger, sadness, nervousness, helplessness?

Name each emotion as it arises, as best as you can and without judging or evaluating it. For example, if you are feeling fear, name it "fear," without judging whether the fear is valid, reasonable, good, or bad. Continue to note and name each strong emotion as you observe it in the remembered conflict. If at any time the emotions seem too overwhelming, come back to your home base, which is the breath.

Continue with this exercise until the timer sounds. Then, slowly release your awareness of the conflict, and gently turn your attention back to your breath, back to the present moment, back to your surroundings. You can deeply inhale and exhale to encourage this return to the present.

Now, without entanglement or fanfare, allow yourself to feel a sense of satisfaction, much as you would after completing a challenging undertaking.

 ## *REFLECTION QUESTIONS*

How did you find this exercise?

_____

_____

_____

_____

Were you able to observe the emotions you experienced as you recalled the conflict?

_____

_____

_____

_____

Were you able to identify the emotions you experienced as you recalled the conflict?

_____

_____

_____

_____

How easy or difficult was it to name emotions rather than thoughts, assessments, evaluations, and the like?

_____

_____

_____

_____

Did naming have any effect on you in the present moment as you remembered the conflict?

_____

_____

_____

_____

How easy or difficult was it to refrain from judging, evaluating, or criticizing your experience?

HOW TO WALK MINDFULLY

At Chom Tong Insight Meditation Center in Chaingmai, Thailand, I practiced a dramatically effective naming technique during walking meditation. When distractions draw your attention away from walking, you bring strong awareness to the distracting event and then return awareness to the object of attention. When you are walking outside, there are frequent distractions, so there are many opportunities to practice.

To try the technique yourself, start by finding a relatively quiet area where you can comfortably pace off eight to twelve steps. Some good places to try are your driveway, the office before most others have arrived or after they have left, your basement, a safe footpath or trail at a less busy time, or a track at a local school.

Mindful walking uses a three-step process. First, lift the foot, move it forward, and lower the foot. Continuing in this way, walk the eight to twelve paces in one direction. At the end, bring both feet together; then turn one foot—say, the right foot—out at a ninety-degree angle. Next, bring your left foot to meet the right. Turn the right foot out at a ninety-degree angle again. Bring your left foot to meet the right. Now you are facing the direction you came from. Start walking again, beginning with either foot, lifting the foot, moving it forward, and lowering it. At the end of eight to twelve paces, turn with either foot as before. Your pace should be neither fast—difficult to attain the desired level of awareness—nor slow—the mind becomes too concentrated on walking to practice noticing when the mind's attention has been pulled away.

While walking, lower your eyes somewhat, but for safety, do not look directly down at your feet so that you can maintain some degree of awareness of your external environment. Pay attention to the action of your feet: lifting, forward movement, lowering; lifting, forward movement, lowering. Have your attention to walking be gentle and light, rather than intense. Your mind is not too tight and concentrated, nor is it too loose and dispersed.

WHAT TO DO WHEN DISTRACTED

Distractions pull your attention away from walking and the present. To return, stop walking and notice and name that you are standing in this moment. Name the distraction three times. Then start walking again.

To return to the present when you are distracted, first try to notice whenever something draws your attention away from walking. The distraction could be thoughts, emotions, sounds, smells, sights, or bodily sensations. When distraction happens, stop walking. As you stop, say to yourself three times, "Stopping, stopping, stopping." Then, name the sensation that caused the distraction three times. For example, if you heard a motorcycle pass by you would say, "Hearing, hearing, hearing." Keep naming the sensation as long as the distraction keeps pulling your attention away or until it dissipates. Then, coming back to the present moment, as you are standing there, name it: "Standing, standing, standing." Finally, resume walking. Repeat this process every time your mind is distracted from your attention to walking.

I felt this immersive technique was like an exclamation point around my distractions and returning from them. Standing there, not moving, just saying the words to myself—hearing, hearing, hearing—was a dramatic representation of each time my mind wandered. Just as important, seeing fellow practitioners doing the same thing, a dozen of us stopping and standing still every few seconds, was a testament to our shared human condition—having a mind prone to distraction.

No one is free from a mind that wanders or does not stay on task. Victory goes to those who master the challenge of seeing it happen and become able to wrest control of their minds back from distraction.

Naming during the Heat of Conflict

In mindfulness meditation, such as in the preceding exercises, the principal use of naming is to help return us to mindful awareness. Practicing this technique while sitting on a cushion or in a chair, or during walking meditation, gives us the ability to bring the benefits of the technique to the arena of conflict.

In conflict, naming is effective in reinforcing our ability to see or observe the strong responses that arise. It also builds our ability to maintain some distance from those responses. To see how this works, suppose you are sitting at your office desk working on a project when the phone rings. You look at the caller ID and see that the caller is a direct report with whom you've been having an ongoing disagreement about how much personal time they are taking. When you see who is calling, you have an immediate physical reaction: your jaw clenches, and your shoulders tighten. You think to yourself, "Oh no, not this knucklehead." All of this happens in a millisecond. If you noticed these reactions in real time and named your thinking—perhaps angry thoughts—and your bodily sensations—perhaps clenching—how might your attitude shift before you picked up the phone? Would you laugh at your reaction as very human and relax a bit?

Or suppose you are about to go into a performance review with a direct report or subordinate who you suspect, based on past experiences, may become belligerent. If you checked in with what was happening internally and named it—perhaps fear—how might the information change how you approached the meeting? Would you seek support? Would you respond to the employee differently? For example, perhaps you would respond with gentle suggestions, rather than dictate as a way to overcompensate for the fear.

The act of naming can help us be with these difficult emotions and sensations without drowning in them. An important part of the technique is adopting a gentle, nonjudging, noncriticizing tone when noting and naming. Act like you're talking to a dear friend and seeing what they're going through, naming their experience. The purpose of naming is not to engage in one more head trip; it is not one more opportunity to beat ourselves up. The purpose is to clarify, not entangle ourselves with, an emotion, thought, or behavior.

Many psychologists suggest that these thoughts, emotions, and bodily sensations are not inherently good or bad, negative or positive. Rather they are natural and provide useful information that helps us be more aware of our inner state. Our response to thoughts, emotions, and sensations—perhaps especially our response to emotions that we consider negative—cause us much trouble. The emotions themselves do not cause trouble, problems, or suffering; our reactions to them and what we do with them cause the problems. And the trouble or destructive behavior begins when we resist, turn away from, repress, push away, or otherwise try to run away from emotions.

After Naming Comes Acceptance

Managers dealing with conflict too often choose responses that look like avoidance and denial, rejecting the thoughts, emotions, and sensations that arise. It is a figurative and literal turning away from conflict, and the trigger is usually fear.

But when we name—especially emotions, which conflict management techniques typically do not attend to—we plant the seeds to be with our feelings without identifying with them so closely that we confuse them with who we are. Instead of running away from them, we note them. By noting them, we open the door to accepting them. And this brings us closer to working with them in more skillful, wiser ways.

We take up the skill of acceptance in the next chapter.

CHAPTER FOUR

Accept It—How to Be with Conflict as It Is, Not How We Wish It Would Be

The first step toward change is awareness.
The second step is acceptance.

—NATHANIEL BRANDEN, PIONEERING PSYCHOTHERAPIST
IN THE FIELD OF SELF-ESTEEM

After nearly two days of travel, I finally arrived in India. I was excited and anxious about immersing myself in yogic philosophy in the country where it all began.

I knew that India would be unlike any other country I had visited, yet I could not have imagined I would feel so thoroughly overwhelmed by the experience. Every sense felt under assault by the sights, sounds, and smells. People were crushed into every conceivable space. The poverty was acute and in plain sight. Motorcycles, tuk tuks, cars, and cows shared the roads. Hawkers, horns, and the sounds of daily living in the open were overpowering.

Peace seemed impossible. And every cell in my body resisted. How could I stay here? How could I learn something about inner peace and calm here? Stepping into this wildly chaotic scene was painful enough. My mind's resistance to this new reality doubled down on my suffering. After many days of watching what my mind was doing and reflecting on how its thinking added to my unhappiness, gradually I was able to loosen the grip of resistance. Slowly, slowly, I came to see that the forces at work were much larger than me, that I was not the center of the universe, and that, over the millennia, millions of Indians had found peace and happiness in this land of extremes.

Letting go of my resistance helped me get curious and investigate how humans can come to accept with equanimity being with such difficulty. In those few months, I began to learn something about how accepting the unpleasant didn't mean I had to like it. I could be with it in a way that promoted greater peace and less misery.

Accepting Conflict as Is

One of the most challenging aspects to any behavioral transformation—and life itself—is learning how to accept the way things are right now. When we don't accept the way things are, we short circuit our present experience and make the journey to change and of life more difficult. Instead of accepting the difficulties in our workplace or personal lives, we often reject them, and that rejection is the source of suffering and confusion.

Accepting the way things are becomes an issue only in difficult times. We are content to accept experiences that bring us happiness—

praise for a job well done, a promotion, a favorable performance evaluation, a raise. Like a lover experiencing the thrall of a first romance, we grasp and cling to those experiences, wanting them to never go and trying to replicate them over and over.

But whether pleasant or unpleasant, experiences don't last. So grasping and craving for pleasant experiences to remain or trying to reproduce them can lead to frustration. We saw this with the COVID pandemic of 2020 when state governments required many shops to close in the beginning weeks. For many people, the ordinary routine of getting coffee at their favorite coffee shop had become so ritualized and pleasant that the inability to relive the experience came with a profound sense of loss. When we reject what is in favor of how we want things to be or how we think things should be, we create unnecessary suffering for ourselves.

NO ONE WANTS TO ACCEPT CONFLICT

Learning to accept negative or unpleasant experiences is a difficult mindset for us humans to adopt. Who wants to accept conflict, for goodness' sake? For one thing, dealing with conflict takes time. Most people would rather be doing what we think is more productive work, although conflict, handled well, can be productive, yielding more creative solutions and teams who feel better connected. Conflict is messy. During my legal work representing the Federal Bureau of Prisons in employment matters, wardens often told me that they would rather deal with murderous inmates than employee problems. Conflicts are not tidy and subject to neat resolutions. Often at the beginning of a conflict, a clear solution might not readily appear to us. Conflict also takes physical, mental, and emotional energy and can feel depleting.

Perhaps most significantly, dealing with conflict means that we might have to confront patterns of our behavior that we would rather not look at too carefully. These cognitive, behavioral, and emotional patterns are often hidden and unconscious. For example, we might think that we always need to be right or are, in fact, always right. Another person might feel responsible for everything that goes wrong. Both these positions put the individual's ego at the center, and who wants to think of themselves as being egotistical?

Given the downsides, it is understandable that we resist conflict. Yet, denying that conflict exists is like pretending we are not getting wet when we are caught in a storm and rain is pouring down on our heads. Conflict is part of reality and part of the human experience.

Acceptance doesn't mean resignation/capitulation.

—MICHAEL J. FOX, ACTOR, AUTHOR, AND ACTIVIST

Resistance Increases Our Suffering

Ironically, the psychological resistance we bring to conflict increases our suffering. When we experience a difficult situation, that experience alone can be painful, and that pain warrants our attention, respect, and compassion. When we fall and break a leg, we feel physical and mental pain. This ability to feel pain has a beneficial effect because it helps to keep us safe and avoid harmful situations. For example, if we break a leg because we were skiing faster than was safe and did not see a rock, we're likely to slow down and pay better attention to our surroundings when the cast comes off.

Likewise, the pain we experience from conflict teaches us something. Perhaps we disagreed with a colleague during a meeting and yelled. The consequences might range from losing a valued collegial relationship to extended conflict with teammates to a conversation with human resources. In any case, if we pay attention, the pain will help us choose a behavior other than yelling in the future.

Often, an additional element accompanies pain: we tell ourselves stories about the pain we're experiencing. We might admonish ourselves for always being too impatient or aggressive because that inclination contributed to our fall on the ski slope and the broken leg. Conversely, we might seek to blame external factors such as the interference of bad skiers. The story is what we say to ourselves about the unpleasant experience we are having, and it sits atop the unpleasant experience itself.

When it comes to workplace conflict, we might engage in negative storytelling, such as saying that we are stupid, bad, or poor managers for having to deal with conflict or for how we respond to conflict, such as by avoiding it. Spiritual teachers speak of the two arrows. Someone shoots the first arrow; you are struck, and that produces pain. For example, the fact that conflict has arisen is the first arrow. The second arrow is the story you tell about the first arrow, and that story produces even more pain. The second arrow might be how you deny or resist the fact that this conflict has arisen. Having yelled at a colleague during a meeting is embarrassing. Telling ourselves how stupid we were for doing so makes the pain worse.

Psychotherapist Peter Michaelson says:

> *Psychological resistance is an aspect of human nature that not only forms an inner barrier but also causes people to act against their best interests. Under the influence of such resistance, we decline to shift away from our negative emotions, to change our bad habits, to initiate plans and strategies for self-fulfillment, and to open our minds to more objective consideration of our perceptions and beliefs.*[1]

The Meaning of Acceptance

Nearly all the ideas we associate with acceptance are misconceptions of its true meaning. When we are better able to accept conflict with all its turmoil and messiness, we open the door to individual change and transformation and step through to more skillful dispute resolution. However, the practice of acceptance can be subtle, not easily grasped, and can take some time to get comfortable with and skillful in. Yet once we learn to be with unpleasantness or discomfort without reflexively trying to get rid of it, we see what is there and accept it for what it is. Then, we can be with conflict and our uncomfortable emotional responses to it with less struggle, avoidance, and fear and with greater resilience and strength. This is a radically different approach from how we deal with difficulty now.

TOWARD A DEFINITION OF ACCEPTANCE IN CONFLICT

When we set aside our many misconceptions, we can explore what acceptance during conflict means. Acceptance is the mental quality of being with an experience without resistance. It is important on the path to increased resilience in conflict because before we can change our behavior, we have to understand fully what we're dealing with. Learning how to accept a conflict experience without resistance is important in getting to understand what internal and external experiences are arising.

ACCEPTING DOESN'T MEAN CAPITULATION

When we think about accepting unpleasant circumstances, we are unlikely to equate anything positive with the idea. We think of acceptance as having to like our situation, as capitulation, resignation, or giving up. This is not what acceptance means. The Buddhist writer and teacher Jack Kornfield puts it nicely: "Acceptance allows us to relax and open up to the facts before us. It does not mean that we cannot work to improve things. But just now, this is what is so."[2]

The distinction between resignation and acceptance combined with a willingness to improve things was aptly demonstrated by divergent approaches to the problem of corruption during my time in Afghanistan. When I was an advisor to Afghan policy makers at the Ministry of Defense and later at the Ministry of Labor (MOLSAMD), we had a recurring and increasingly urgent conversation about corruption among Afghan officials. It was a significant and ongoing problem, well documented by international organizations. The problem of corruption was deep, multifaceted, and controversial. Afghanistan's then-president Hamid Karzai publicly accused Western nations of laying the groundwork for, and the proliferation of, corruption. Sometimes there were no bright lines for what constituted corruption. For example, most would agree that paying a bribe at the border to ensure your goods got through was not a legitimate business practice. On the other hand, not everyone agreed that members of a tribe in influential government positions reaching back and helping other tribe members gain employment—without the benefit of competition and without consideration of merit—constituted a form of corruption that warranted uprooting. After all, many nations engage in this latter practice to some extent.

American military leaders understood these complexities well. I have no doubt that NATO allies did also. They both accepted that this was the current reality, an undeniable feature of the present landscape. Yet some, including the Americans, sought to take steps for change, concluding that such corruption was too destructive to warrant allowing it to continue. They accepted the current reality in a realistic and full way while still advocating for change. Other allies, however, thought such corruption was a cost of doing business in Afghanistan that should be accepted as such without mounting any real change effort. This is resignation. The difference means a society in which mistrust in the government's ability to execute fundamental governmental activities and employ competent government officials is allowed to fester versus deliberately working to help build a government in which ordinary Afghans have a level of trust that the government is there for them rather than only for a select cadre of the well connected.

Acceptance, standing in contrast to resignation, has a nuanced meaning and encompasses a broader attitude. But in some cultures, people view accepting reality as it is in the moment as a kind of settling. In fact, recently I heard a popular American motivational speaker with a significant online following say that we should never accept our current situation, no matter what it is. Most of us are always striving for something better or more, whether through self-improvement or accumulating material things.

I used to believe this also: that I should never be satisfied with my present circumstances, even when they might be objectively wonderful. In fact, Grant, my law school roommate, commented that it must be very difficult to live having such an attitude. He was right; it was difficult. In my twenties especially, I lived in a perpetual state of constant striving for some ill-defined, amorphous goal, which left me feeling unhappy and dissatisfied with whatever was happening in the present moment, no matter how wonderful it might have been. In Buddhist thought this is called *dukkha*. It wasn't until many years later that I began to understand the corrosive, thoroughly unhelpful impact that this inability to accept the way things are—even for a moment—had in my life.

WITH ACCEPTANCE, WE STRUGGLE LESS IN CONFLICT

With acceptance in conflict, we acknowledge that conflict happens, and it is unpleasant; acceptance is merely a statement about the way things are. This attitude is similar to how many people view weather: rain happens, we don't control where or when, and it's folly to struggle against it.

When we better understand the true nature of how we respond to conflict and manage it, we are in a much better place to decide—with wisdom—how we want to effect change. Too often when it comes to our own personal development and transformation, we bypass this step of accepting things for how they really are and instead try to learn the technique or strategy we think will help us get out of our mess. Taking shortcuts like this doesn't work. When I first started working with contemplative practices to ease my suffering and develop a sense of true contentment, I had the tendency to bypass the sometimes-tough dealing-with-my-emotions phase and jump right to the this-is-me-calm-and-contented stage.

Trying to bypass the important developmental step of acceptance leads us to repress or deny our emotions, rather than acknowledge and deal with them in an open way. That was the case with me. Psychologist, Zen priest, and teacher Tim Burkett talks about the suffering that comes from difficult or tragic circumstances and says that "[t]ouching the heart that suffers and staying with it is the most difficult thing we do as human beings."[3] He says that we cannot bypass the acceptance of our emotions on the way to cultivating greater awareness and openness toward them (rather than the shutting down that often attends them). Taking such shortcuts, trying to get directly to the brass ring, he says, makes us brittle and cold. For example, becoming aware of strong emotions arising in conflict but going straight to strategies to calm the body without first accepting the reality of those strong emotions does not promote a healthy integration of those emotions. Instead, moving directly to calming the body leads to repression or denial of those strong emotions. As John Welwood, associate editor of the *Journal of Transpersonal Psychology* and former director of the East/West psychology program at the California Institute of Integral Studies, points out, we can use ideas or practices "to sidestep or avoid facing unresolved emotional issues, psychological wounds, and unfinished developmental tasks."[4] Welwood was speaking of spiritual bypass, but the concept is no less relevant here.

Acceptance Is the Pathway to Happiness and Equanimity

The practice of acceptance as a pathway to happiness, well-being, and equanimity is a prevalent theme in Western psychology, in Buddhist philosophy, and in various religions and philosophies. For example, acceptance is a fundamental tenet of the twelve-step Alcoholics Anonymous program. The program's basic text, *Alcoholics Anonymous*, often called simply *The Big Book*, includes the following passage: "Acceptance is the answer to all my problems today. When I am disturbed, it is because I find some person, place, thing or situation—some fact of my life—unacceptable to me. I can find no serenity until I accept that person, place, thing or situation as being exactly the way it is supposed to be at this moment."[5]

In his book *Mindfulness in Plain English*, the Buddhist monk Bhante H. Gunaratana writes:

> *Meditation is running straight into reality. It does not insulate you from the pain of life but rather allows you to delve so deeply into life and all its aspects that you pierce the pain barrier and go beyond suffering … In order to observe our fear, we must*

accept the fact that we are free. We can't examine our own depression without accepting it fully. The same is true for irritation, agitation, frustration and all those other uncomfortable emotional states. You can't examine something fully if you were busy rejecting its existence.[6]

Thich Nhat Hanh, recipient of the World Peace Forum's Luxembourg Peace Prize in 2019, nominated for the Nobel Peace Prize by Dr. Martin Luther King Jr., in 1967, and world-renowned for his highly engaged Buddhist approach, observing the normality of fear, wrote that "Fear is always there within us … It is very human to be fearful and to worry about it."[7] However, Hanh also recognized that resisting a difficult emotion such as fear is unhelpful. He pointed out, "If you try to run away, instead of confront or embracing your ill-being, you will not look deeply into its nature and will never have the chance to see a way out. That is why you should hold your suffering tenderly and closely, looking directly into it to discover its true nature and find a way out."[8]

Acceptance has more to offer than helping us suffer less. It also leads to resilience. In their book *Resilience: The Science Behind Mastering Life's Greatest Challenges*, coauthors Drs. Steven Southwick and Dennis Charney chronicle their extensive study of resilient people—people like prisoners of war or survivors of other tremendously traumatic events. They were looking for patterns, common factors that contribute to individuals' resilience. They observed that many individuals who were able to overcome incredible trauma and difficulty "cited acceptance as critical in their ability to thrive under conditions of high stress and trauma."[9]

Even if it does not happen readily or easily, accepting being in a difficult situation also maintains or enhances well-being. For example, a nationwide survey after the September 11, 2001, terrorist attacks showed that individuals who accepted the situation experienced lower levels of post-traumatic stress symptoms.[10]

By reducing suffering, supporting well-being, and building resilience, acceptance is a stepping stone toward happiness, or at least toward equanimity and strength in the face of the difficult experiences and emotions that life throws our way.

> *By reducing suffering, supporting well-being, and building resilience, acceptance is a stepping stone toward happiness, or at least toward equanimity and strength in the face of the difficult experiences and emotions that life throws our way.*

Acceptance, however, doesn't seem to come naturally. We are more likely to find difficulties unacceptable, be fearful, and run away from difficult emotions. How do we strengthen our capacity to work with this resistance and better accept our current reality?

Strengthening the Capacity to Work with Acceptance

Conflict is one of the most difficult situations we encounter in our work lives. How can we better stand in conflict with courage, just being with whatever arises, without running away, denying, or rejecting it? The answers lie in strategies grounded in mindfulness and cognitive restructuring or reappraisal.

In the following exercise, we are building resilience, the mental and psychological ability to understand and accept uncomfortable emotions without running away. By doing so, we move closer to working with conflict and our responses to it more skillfully and wisely.

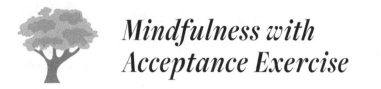

Mindfulness with Acceptance Exercise

For this exercise, you will need some time when you are not too tired, sleepy, or distracted by life to concentrate, a timer placed within arm's reach, a chair or cushion, and a relatively quiet space.

Read the entire section before beginning.

After reading the instructions, sit on a chair, a cushion, or on the floor in a position so that your body is grounded, balanced, comfortable, and alert. When ready, if you are new to mindfulness, set the timer for five minutes.

Set an intention for the session to pay attention to what is happening inside, as it happens, in a nonjudging, compassionate way. For example, you might state your intention as, "With kindness toward myself, I am sitting to gain insight into my way of showing up with respect to accepting conflict so that I may be of greater benefit to myself and others." Feel free to create your own intention that is wholesome, not overly ambitious, and aligned with the aims of the practice. Then start the timer.

Allow your body to feel relaxed. Try to generate a sense of open awareness and receptivity, as if you were in the presence of a trusted teacher or loving friend. Though your body is relaxed and open, let your mind be alert and curious, as though you were reading a page-turner of a book.

Turn your attention to your breathing. Focus on the place in your body where you most readily and deeply connect to your breath. For most, that's the belly or chest. Let your breath be your anchor.

As you breathe in, notice how the belly or chest rises as the breath moves into your body. As you breathe out, notice how the belly or chest falls as the breath leaves your body. Follow the entire breathing cycle. As you breathe in, notice the pause at the top of the breath; as you breathe out, notice the pause at the bottom of the breath. Don't manipulate the breath by consciously slowing it down or holding it. Simply observe your breath with a gentle, present, open awareness. With gentleness and open awareness, simply observe as you breathe in and out.

Continue observing your breath until you get some sense of steadiness or stability, even if slight or fleeting. This might take a few minutes.

Next, as in previous exercises, visualize a time when you were in a work-related conflict with someone. The conflict should not be of great intensity or scope. If you cannot identify a work-related conflict, choose one from another area of your life. Whether work-related or from some other area of life, choose a conflict that has caused you some suffering but does not pose an existential threat.[11]

After you have the conflict in mind, gently turn your awareness away from your breath and to the remembered conflict. Be as specific as you can in recalling the details of the conflict. Where did the conflict take place? Whom were you with? How did the conflict arise? How is it unfolding? What are you saying? What are others saying? What is the tone and body language like? Try to see yourself and others as clearly as possible in the conflict. If this visualization is difficult, do not worry about it. Try to generate a feeling of being in the conflict, even if it is amorphous. Even if you cannot see the event clearly, see if you can get a feel for the tone of the experience.

Now, remembering the conflict as vividly as you can and having some feeling of what it was like being in it, using the naming technique that you learned in the last chapter, name the strong emotions that arise. For example, if you are feeling hatred toward the other person, name it "hatred." Is it fear? Anger? Overwhelm? Inadequacy? Describe what the emotion feels like. For example, perhaps it feels heavy, stuck, or hard. Where in your body do you feel this emotion the strongest? Your stomach? Chest? Shoulders? Jaw? Continue naming, describing, and locating as strong emotions arise.

If at any time they seem too overwhelming, come back to your home base, which is the breath.

Now try to get a sense of what you might be accepting or rejecting about this experience. What resistance might you be experiencing? Even if it doesn't feel strong, observe it, like a detective, to detect even the subtlest sense of rejection or pushing away. What do you want to turn away from? What feels uncomfortable? What do you find most difficult about being in the situation? See both the discomfort and the way you want to turn away from it. You are not trying to manipulate or change anything. You are just trying to get to know yourself and the way you are in conflict.

As you do this exercise, refrain from judging or criticizing your experience. Like you would with a dear friend in distress, just be with yourself with care and compassion.

Continue the exercise until the timer sounds. Then, slowly release your awareness of the conflict, and gently turn your attention back to your breath, back to the present moment, back to your surroundings. You can deeply inhale and exhale to encourage this return.

Without entanglement or fanfare, congratulate yourself as you would a dear friend for undertaking a challenging project. Out of all the things tugging at your time and attention, you chose to devote your energy to training and developing your mind, which will benefit you, your colleagues, subordinates, superiors, direct reports, and those to whom you report.

REFLECTION QUESTIONS

How did you feel about this exercise? I found this exercise:

_____

_____

_____

_____

What, if anything, felt uncomfortable? I felt most uncomfortable when:

_____

_____

_____

_____

What aspects of the conflict or your response to it did you find hard to accept? I found it hard to accept:

_____

_____

_____

_____

What stories did you tell yourself about the conflict or your response to it? I noticed I would tell stories about:

_____

_____

_____

_____

What aspects of the conflict or your response to it did you want to turn away from or resist? I noticed I resisted when:

_____

_____

_____

_____

What aspects of this exercise did you gain insight from or were surprising? I gained the most insight from or was most surprised when:

_____

_____

_____

_____

What about engaging with this exercise are you most proud of? I am most proud of myself for:

_____

_____

_____

_____

Practicing Acceptance during the Heat of Conflict

When we sit in formal practice on our meditation chair or cushion, our mindfulness practice encourages us to accept whatever arises, whether fun thoughts, negative thoughts, fantasies, pain, restlessness, calm, sadness, and all the rest. When we do so, we are building our capacity for resilience. This helps us when we are in the real deal—when actual conflict arises. With practice, we can be in conflict without running away. This, in turn, helps us avoid engaging in unskillful actions because of our habitual, unconscious patterns of behavior.

But how do we "do" acceptance in an actual conflict situation? Suppose an employee who reports to you walks into your office to request time off, a seemingly straightforward request. However, you have challenges with this particular employee because they don't come to work on time, frequently call out sick at the last minute, and clock watch in the afternoon. So although you were sitting at your desk writing a report, feeling relatively at ease, when John walks into your office, your mindfulness practice helps you become aware that your jaw clenches a little and your stomach tightens a bit.

As John unabashedly makes his request, the mindfulness training you learned in Chapter 2 kicks in, helping you become more aware of your thoughts. You might become aware that you think, "I don't believe this guy. I know for a fact that he's been in the office only six days in the last two weeks. Now he has the nerve to ask for vacation time off. This is the laziest, most no-account employee I've ever had. He avoids doing work if he can. I don't know why I didn't fire him a long time ago. In fact, he still hasn't given me his team's progress report that was due five days ago. I ought to go down to human resources right now and see what I can do to get rid of this guy. I'm sick of his nonsense." You notice that your predominant thought at the moment is that you are sick of the guy's nonsense. You are seeing what is developing right before your eyes, integrating the awareness practice you learned in Chapter 2. Inwardly, you smile.

Figuring you're on a roll, you work with naming and identify your predominant thoughts and feelings as resentment, tension, disgust, and anger. You also notice that as the conflict builds, you are in danger of striking out in your habitual patterns—sarcasm, flippancy, and hostility. You reflect that this pattern of behavior has probably contributed to your poor relationship with John, even though your business concerns are justified.

After noting that the situation is leading to conflict—this is where acceptance comes into play—you accept that John is asking for vacation time and isn't the most dedicated employee on the team. You become curious. You wonder if he is aware that he has been out of the office a lot over the past few weeks. You also wonder whether he's aware of the impression he makes by not coming to work on time, calling out sick at the last minute, and clock watching. You wonder how you could wonder—surely, he must know what he's doing? Slowly your jaw begins to unclench, and your stomach begins to loosen. And instead of lashing out, you ask John what's been up with him.

When we can mindfully recognize and accept how unpleasant a situation is and how uncomfortable we are in it, we can reduce our discomfort. And when we reduce our discomfort, we can bring a resourceful attitude to working with conflict. With self-compassion, like a loving parent would respond to a child who was injured or hurt, so, too, do we bring an attitude of gentleness and care. Mindfulness, the path of seeing, carries this very important element.

Acceptance must be actively practiced. It isn't a passive process. But each time you accept things as they are, you create and strengthen neural pathways in your brain—you create a habit—making each subsequent time a little bit easier. You can practice acceptance anytime, anywhere.

Acceptance must be actively practiced. It isn't a passive process.

As thoughts, emotions, and sensations arise, say, "It is what it is." It is possible that by acknowledging these emotions and leaning into, allowing, and opening to them that the experience itself begins to change. Naming helps with acceptance. So does curiosity. Opening up to feelings comes from curiosity, for example, asking: Where did this feeling come from? Where do I feel it? What is good about it? What is its nature and quality? Is it changing as I observe it? Even though feelings might change as you accept them, the aim of acknowledging is not to try to get rid of them.

REFRAMING FEAR

Another technique for cultivating acceptance is to create an alternative story about the difficult emotion or negative event with a more positive meaning. By using a positive meaning to build context for what is difficult, an individual reframes the experience and makes acceptance more attainable.

A powerful reframing technique views difficult events and emotions, particularly conflict, as opportunities for learning and growth. This reframing of events is an aspect of resilience. As Southwick and Charney point out, "The capacity to positively reframe and extract meaning from adversity is an important component of stress resilience: resilient individuals often find that trauma has forced them to learn something new or to grow as a person."[12] Individuals who are better able to reframe traumatic events experience a wide range of benefits such as "greater compassion for and acceptance of others; ... a greater sense of kinship with humanity; ... development of more effective coping skills; ... improved self-esteem and self-respect; and enhanced wisdom and maturity."[13] They state, "In sum, people who are resilient tend to be flexible [cognitively]: they know when to accept that which cannot be changed and how to positively reframe life's challenges and failures."[14]

Moving from Resistance to Acceptance and Beyond

When conflict, difficult emotions, or challenging events occur, we have two choices: reject or resist the reality or accept it. When we reject or resist reality, we add suffering to our difficulties. Often, what underlies our resistance is a fear or mistaken belief that when we accept reality, whatever it may be, we are approving it, endorsing it, or even liking it. It is worth repeating that acceptance does not mean that we have to like what is arising. Soto Zen priest and founder of the Bright Way Zen community Domyo Burk points out that acceptance is distinctly different from liking what is: "Do you see how this has nothing to do with twisting your experience around and pretending you think all the misery in the world is actually beautiful? It doesn't deny or sanitize or reinterpret your experience. It doesn't say anything about what you're going to do *next*. It's entirely about being fully present *right now*."[15]

Acceptance is also not a stance of capitulation or resignation to the unpleasant situation that confronts us. It does not carry a sense of waving the white flag of surrender. However, ceasing to fight the resistance that we normally bring to a negative experience—rather than outright submit to it—can be a valuable step toward a transition to acceptance. Spiritual philosopher Eckhart Tolle talks about surrender as the inner transition from resistance to acceptance, from "no" to "yes." He also discusses the pain that we create for ourselves when we are in conflict with and resistant to external circumstances at any given moment. This gets to the heart of the matter: when we have a negative experience and resist it and the emotions it brings, we end up with pain and suffering on top of the negative experience. When we practice acceptance, we have only the negative experiences, difficult emotions, and maybe pain. Suffering is optional.

With the mindfulness techniques that you learned in Chapter 2, you can now better bring intentional awareness to circumstances that likely give rise to conflict, as well as your habitual style of responding to it. Having seen what is arising, you used the naming practices in Chapter 3 to identify your emotional responses—for example, fear— to the developing conflict. And naming may have tamped down the intensity of your emotions. In this chapter, we looked clear eyed at this fear or other challenging emotions, recognized the discomfort, and refused to turn away. We learned to accept conflict and our emotions while honoring the difficulty with self-kindness.

Each time we find ourselves in a difficult spot, we can approach it with curiosity, asking questions such as these: What do I want to turn away from right now? What is making it difficult for me to stay in this moment? What do I find most difficult about being in this situation? With curiosity, we can learn about our situation and accept it.

In the throes of intense conflict, an acceptance practice is challenging. Starting with smaller difficulties, we can practice, gradually building up the strength to use this strategy with bigger conflicts.

While we have been learning and honing skills on the cushion, we also understand that we cannot leave them there. We have to bring them into the world we live in—the world of conflict. By continually strengthening our skills in mindfully seeing, naming, and accepting, we are positioning ourselves to stand in conflict with greater strength and act with greater wisdom. This increased awareness allows us to gain better control over our responses to conflict. Pausing is one such powerful technique that helps us do so. We'll learn how in the next chapter.

CHAPTER FIVE

Pause It—How to Make Space for Doing Something New

It's a transformative experience to simply pause instead of immediately filling up space.

—PEMA CHÖDRÖN, BUDDHIST TEACHER, AUTHOR, AND NUN

W e were mingling, talking in hushed voices at the back of the classroom at the end of another class on Buddhist philosophy. Practitioners like me and Buddhist nuns had been living and studying at the retreat center in northern India for many weeks, and some for months or years. The lessons, taught by a Tibetan monk and translated by a young Russian woman, were provocative and difficult and usually left me with many questions, which we were encouraged to ask.

Suddenly, the "mean nun" approached me as I stood talking with some classmates. I did not think this would be a positive experience. Few with the mean nun were, as some of us students had given her the appellation because of her seemingly permanent scowl and brusque, by-the-book manner. We stopped talking. Looking at me, she asked if I could "shut up and stop asking questions during the class." She found my questions disruptive and simply wanted to hear the teacher's lessons without any interruptions.

By this time, I had been meditating and doing the inner work for some years. In that instant, it seemed like I saw all of the mean nun's pain. There was genuine distress in her eyes. And having spent enough time in East Asian countries by then, I knew that in-the-moment analysis and critical thinking were often not prioritized above rote learning and memorization in many of them, and the mean nun was of an age and cultural background where that was likely true for her. I was able to gain some distance from the request. My immediate reaction was not to personalize it or take it as some fundamental failure in myself. All of this went through my mind very, very quickly.

I paused and took all of this in, in that moment. In that pause I was even able to see how I had not automatically reacted with anger or insult. In that pause I felt a sense of control. I marveled at that. For an instant, I truly felt freedom from being enslaved by emotion. I felt like all of my work had paid off. And it had.

Without any feeling of malice or sarcasm, I told the mean nun I would think about her request. And I did.

We've been exploring what we think, sense, and feel when we're engaged in the difficult experience of conflict. The first step was learning how to see and be present for what is going on in any life situation. Seeing our thoughts, sensations, and emotions in the present moment is the antidote to living in a trance, captivated by past experiences, plans, or any random thought. Second, we learned to name our thoughts, feelings, and sensations as a technique to develop our focus on the present moment. An additional benefit of naming is that it calms and helps us maintain balance and stability in the face of intense emotions. Accepting conflict as it is and the powerful thoughts, sensations, and emotions that arise as they are bolsters our ability to approach conflict with confidence and stand in conflict with strength and wisdom.

You might wonder, "If I've already taken the time to See, Name, and Accept, doesn't it go without saying that I have Paused?" Pausing means something slightly more than that. For a moment, think about what conflict feels like. If you go into a situation believing there is a potential for conflict, you may feel keyed up, your senses on high alert and your mind evaluating strategies. You might not be in full fight-flight-freeze mode, but you're ready for action—hypervigilant and reactive. The practice of seeing, naming, and accepting makes you aware of these states. Pausing at this moment creates some space between the self who sees, names, and accepts and the self who reacts out of habit. In that moment, you have time to appreciate what is arising, time to be curious, and a better chance to choose a wise response.

I've emphasized throughout how important it is to practice these skills to build your mental muscles. The exercises in which you visualize, using See It, Name It, and Accept It during a past conflict, help build your capacity to draw on them in the midst of conflict. Why is practice so important? The thoughts, emotions, and sensations that arise do so in an instant. Seeing, Naming, and Accepting don't come naturally. A deliberate pause slows things down so that you can more effectively See, Name, and Accept.

Habitual Responses to Conflict Arise at the Speed of Thought

In the preceding chapter, we worked with how to understand and practice accepting strong emotions, thoughts, or sensations that might arise when we are in a difficult spot. We considered the common problem of a low-performing employee asking for time off. In that hypothetical situation, the manager went from writing a report to thinking about firing the employee in a fraction of a second.

It can take only several milliseconds[1] for an impulse to move from one neuron in the brain to another, just an instant to go from feeling calm to more than annoyed, which is why it is so important that we slow down. Slowing down is good but is not enough. We also need to train our mind to do our will, rather than carry us away like an out-of-control horse.

Slowing down is good but is not enough. We also need to train our mind to do our will, rather than carry us away like an out-of-control horse.

Looking over the manager's shoulder, so to speak, we saw him use mindfulness to become aware of the strong content of reactions in his thoughts and the story he was telling himself ("I'm sick of this guy's nonsense. I should have fired him a long time ago."). He used naming to identify emotions (resentment, disgust, or anger) and sensations (tension). He also noticed that he was in danger of lashing out in a habitual pattern of sarcasm and flippancy. Instead, he accepted that this employee was the least dedicated member of his team and was asking for vacation time. Rather than follow his usual pattern into conflict, he became curious about what was going on with his employee. He accepted the unpleasantness of the situation and engaged in a resourceful approach that relieved his discomfort and redirected his habitual reactionary, unwise behavior.

With mindful awareness, naming, and accepting all the thoughts, emotions, and sensations arising in the situation, the manager is in a better position to pause. When he pauses, he just stops any further outward action. He stops talking, gesturing, or pacing; he stops whatever outward behavior he is engaged in.

Why Pause?

Why pause? We pause to interrupt our patterns. We pause to stop our reactivity.

I attend silent meditation retreats as a way to deepen my practice. After one particular ten-day silent meditation retreat in Thailand, I spoke with one of my fellow attendees. He told me that his teacher recommended that he use the technique of stopping—what I'm calling pausing—when he started spinning stories with his thoughts. Just stop; don't try to unpack or explain it. And then continue with your practice or whatever you were doing. He said he was finding the practice to be very effective.

When we left the example of the employee asking for vacation time, the manager had just stopped all his outward behaviors. By pausing like this, he gives himself time to experience balance and stability. The pause also opens space that holds possibilities. If the manager did not pause, events could unfold as they usually would with irritation, lashing out, and escalating the conflict. However, after he pauses, anything could happen next, and that's the point.

In addition to interrupting patterns or stopping reactivity, there are other good reasons to pause. For example, Renée Zellweger paused for six years at the height of her acting career to take time to assess what she was doing, evaluate whether it aligned with her values and goals, and reconnect with her craft. Businesses sometimes pause production to adjust quality or realign their products with what consumers want.

Pausing in tragic circumstances can have powerful and deeply significant benefits. For example, during World War I, in 1914, British and German troops engaged in a spontaneous truce to celebrate Christmas. Soldiers paused hostilities, set aside their guns, and reconnected with their common humanity, sharing whiskey, chocolate, carols, and soccer games.[2] In the late 1990s and early 2000s, nineteen countries around the world established cease-fires so that children could be immunized against polio and other diseases and civilians could receive food and medical relief.[3] And in 2020, more than 50 percent of countries in armed conflict around the world suspended hostilities to help flatten the curve of the coronavirus pandemic.[4]

Science behind Pausing

When we strategically pause, we begin to develop new habits to respond in new ways rather than with old habitual behaviors, which can be suboptimal. Whether a threat is real, like encountering a bear in the woods, or perceived, like the habitual discomfort conflict provokes, it triggers the fight-flight-freeze response. The fight-flight-freeze response is a biological process, a cascade of physiological events that can be difficult to manage once they begin. However, through pausing and breathing (discussed in Chapter 6), you can gain better control over your mind and body's reactions, whether you perceive events as threats and how you behave once the fight-flight-freeze response starts.

The fight-flight-freeze response is an intricate conversation between different systems in the brain, distinct parts of the nervous system, neurotransmitters and hormones throughout the body, and different organ systems. The key neurotransmitters and hormones are epinephrine and norepinephrine (they are both neurotransmitters and hormones) and cortisol. You are probably familiar with the resulting feelings: your heart beats faster, blood pressure rises, and senses are heightened; you might feel edgy, twitchy, or energized. Many people interpret these feelings as anxiety or fear; others interpret them as excitement.

In the brain, learning, whether through day-to-day experiences or deliberate training, establishes new connections and pathways between neurons through a process called neuroplasticity. When we pause in conflict, we give ourselves the space to learn that there is no threat, and we establish new neural connections, weakening the old neural pathways, which activated the flight-fight-freeze response.[5]

Pausing also helps us learn during the fight-flight-freeze response. If you interpret the feelings as anxiety or fear, you might feel that the experience is harmful. When you pause, you learn that your racing heart, heightened senses, and edgy feelings are not harming you. You also learn that what is happening in your body doesn't last very long if there is no threat and you are safe. It takes only a few seconds to a minute or two for the neurotransmitters and hormones to dissipate, except for cortisol, which may take longer.[6]

Pausing enables us to be in the moment of fight-flight-freeze, notice what is arising, and accept it just as it is. Whether we are reframing what triggers the response, reframing how we interpret the response, or simply sitting with it, the experiences rewire the brain, so to speak, through neuroplasticity. When we learn to pause, we use the brain's capacity for flexibility to train for more deliberate, reflective action.

WHAT TO DO IN THE PAUSE

» Say a mantra

» Pray

» Count to ten

» Consider the other person's perspective

» Use humor

» Imagine what you look like to an outsider

» Reflect that you are not your views, thoughts, or opinions

» Reflect on the question, "How am I contributing to this conflict?"

» Ask, "What am I clinging to right now that is not serving this situation?" and reflect on your answer

» Reflect on the impermanent nature of the conflict, its fluidity, and its transitoriness

» Ask, "Where is the learning in this?"

A Practice for Pausing

We can practice pausing at any time, and the workplace offers opportunities to do so. When you practice, try to bring intentional awareness to your pause—that is, know that you intend to pause. Then, take the pause. Feel free to experiment with the length of your pause. A pause during conflict can be for a second, and this can be enough to give us the much-needed space to gain perspective and regroup. In the course of our larger lives, we might pause for an hour, days, or seasons; a sabbatical is a type of pause.

As you pause, notice what you experience. What stories are you telling yourself? What feelings accompany these stories? How does your body respond to the experience of momentarily stopping? Are you too anxious or restless to, so you resume your activity? See if you can just inhabit this moment, allowing whatever wants to arise, arise.

WAYS TO PRACTICE THE PAUSE IN THE WORKPLACE

» In a boring conference call with no others present, before you start multitasking, pause.

» As a colleague who has no appointment enters your workspace and interrupts your work, pause before you greet him or her.

» When writing a difficult email to a client, before you hit send, pause.

» After hanging up the phone, having had a difficult conversation with a client, pause.

» When anxiety, frustration, or confusion become uncomfortably high while writing a long, complex report, pause.

» Before responding during a feedback discussion with your boss, pause.

PAUSING IN THE HEAT OF CONFLICT

When you are in the heat of conflict, draw on all the skills you've learned thus far in this book. First, bring conscious awareness to the conflict as it develops. That is, know conflict has arisen. To help establish that awareness, name it by saying, "This is conflict." Name whatever else is arising most strongly for you, such as a feeling of fear, a sensation of breathlessness, or thoughts like, "I want to hurt this person," "I just want them to go away," or "I want to be anywhere but here." See if you can open the door to acceptance and allow these feelings, sensations, and thoughts.

Next allow the pause to enter this space. This pause is not a repression of thoughts and feelings, but rather choosing for the moment not to react. Inhabit the pause for as long as you find beneficial.

When you are in the heat of conflict, it is difficult to pause or slow down without having any previous experience. However, we know from neuroscience that our brains are endlessly malleable, and we can restructure them with new experiences. Although pausing will take time before it becomes integrated as a new habit, with practice you will become more comfortable and skillful with it. Being kind to yourself and noting your successes along the way will help you keep working with the technique.

Although pausing will take time before it becomes integrated as a new habit, with practice you will become more comfortable and skillful with it. Being kind to yourself and noting your successes along the way will help you keep working with the technique.

Moving from Pausing to Harnessing the Power of the Breath

The goal of pausing is to interrupt our patterns and reestablish mindfulness during conflict. Pausing also provides a moment of stability and balance; it creates the space for more skillful action. When you pause, you give yourself the time to reach for a balance between your emotional mind and your reasoning mind. With the pause and that balance, you experience standing in conflict with greater resilience, strength, and confidence.

Pausing is a natural part of the mindfulness exercises described in Chapters 2, 3, and 4, which help us practice experiencing life in the here and now. Focusing attention on the breath as an anchor, we noticed the pause at the top of the breath while breathing in and the pause at the bottom of the breath while breathing out. Pausing is as automatic a process as breathing. We simply bring deliberate awareness to the experience. Everyone who practices mindfulness meditation experienced this pause during their first session and continues to notice it every time they practice.

In this chapter, we learned to create a pause consciously. In the next chapter, we learn to harness the power of the breath to help us open the door even wider for wise action.

CHAPTER SIX

Breathe—It Really Does Calm Body and Mind

Regulate the breathing and thereby control the mind.

—B. K. S. IYENGAR, PIONEERING YOGA TEACHER

A small group of us—eight civilians—sat in a room not knowing what was coming next. In the middle of a training program for deployment to Afghanistan, we were on a campus meant to simulate an Afghan town. We knew that this was a weapons exercise, but we had no idea what the exercise would involve.

I sat along with the others, nervously waiting for the lesson to be revealed. I had my pistol secured in its holster on my hip. I had been training with weapons—live fire on a range and simulated convoy attacks using paint pellets—and was doing okay. Yet I was nervous and uncomfortable with whatever this new exercise would be. Finally, it was my turn.

My teacher was one of the most remarkable humans I had ever met. Thomas, a navy SEAL, was equal parts toughness, insight, compassion, and humility. I had tremendous respect for this man who deeply understood the awesome power and responsibility that came with his job and was humbled in the face of it.

So Thomas beckoned me out of the room, closing the door to the remaining students. He explained the mission in this simulation: the offices in which I was advising my soon-to-be-clients, Afghan officials at the Afghanistan Ministry of Defense, had come under attack. My job was to get from one end of the corridor of offices to the other end, clearing the space of insurgents who might pop up along the way—in other words, take out the bad guys with my weapon and get to safety at the other end. "Are you kidding me?" I said to myself. I'm a lawyer, not a soldier. I thought, not for the first time, "What the hell am I doing? I volunteered for this mission? I must be nuts." I was terrified, even though I knew none of the bad guys would have weapons and no one would actually be shooting at me.

My first thought was to breathe. I immediately started deep belly breathing, which helped me focus on the task at hand. All distractions fell away as I became completely present to that moment. I unholstered my weapon, took the safety off, and chambered one of the paint-pellet rounds. Thomas took the lead, and I crouched behind him to his right. We fast walked down the hallway, our heads swiveling left and right, looking for bad guys.

Afterward, I couldn't tell you how many bad guys there were or how many I "shot." Thomas didn't tell me either. But what he did say confirmed the power that I knew my steady meditation practice was yielding. He said that he wouldn't have believed it by looking at me (he spoke more politely than this). "But you were completely in the zone, and I haven't seen very many folks approach this exercise with the focus, calm, and deliberation you did." This was high praise coming from a Navy SEAL.

I am not advocating learning or practicing meditation for the purpose of sharpening our ability to do others harm. This couldn't be further from the principle of *ahimsa* (nonharm) associated with meditation's true teachings and purpose. And the question of what the right action is when others seek to harm us is a philosophical question, the discussion of which we must leave for another time. But in this instance, the breath was my savior. While few of us reading this book will have to fight to stay alive, the way we live is often like a simulated fight for survival. The breath can be our savior, giving us that space to approach our lives with greater calm and deliberateness.

What's Breathing Got to Do with It?

When you're agitated, as most of us are when in conflict, having someone tell you to breathe is about as irritating as having someone tell you to calm down. It sounds like a cliché, and besides, you're already breathing.

The diaphragm sits beneath the lungs and above the organs of the abdomen. It separates the two cavities of the torso and attaches to the base of the ribs, the spine, and the sternum. When you are relaxed and inhale, the diaphragm moves down and out to pull air into your lungs and your chest doesn't move much. That's why your belly moves out when you take a breath. See for yourself. Put one hand on your diaphragm and the other on your chest. Breathe without putting effort into it, letting the diaphragm do the work. Feel the motion of your belly, and notice how your chest hardly moves at all.

However, how you breathe during the heightened arousal of a fight-flight-freeze response (also known as the stress response) is often different from how you usually breathe, and the differences have a profound impact on body and mind. When a real or perceived threat triggers the fight-flight-freeze response, as often happens during conflict, your breath becomes shallow and rapid. This gets oxygen to your muscles more quickly, so you are prepared to confront the threat. However, repeatedly responding in this way creates a habit whereby we automatically respond to conflict with this type of rapid breathing.

Shallow breathing may send a signal to the body that it is under stress. When breathing is shallow, we use the muscles in the chest, shoulders, and neck to breathe instead of letting the diaphragm do the work. This creates tension, which also contributes to stress. Thus, an unhealthy cycle is created. But just as mindfulness helps you break away from the autopilot habit, consciously engaging the breath helps you trigger the relaxation response.

If you develop a practice of deep breathing, over time instead of breathing shallowly when the fight-flight-freeze response is triggered, you can immediately access this skill of taking deep, long breaths. Deep breathing helps calm the body and mind. Being able to draw on that skill almost as automatically as taking a breath itself will help you stand in the storm of conflict with greater equilibrium and confidence.

Conflict Takes Many Forms and Happens Fast

It does not take much at work to shift from focusing on drafting a report, writing a piece of programming code, or running a safety check to feeling anxious and then to being in full fight-flight-freeze mode. A difficult meeting, interruption while you're concentrating, poor performance review, or disagreement with a coworker or manager is not a physical danger, like a wild animal, out-of-control car, or armed conflict, but it still elicits the fight-flight-freeze response. It is the same response to threat that enabled our ancestors to survive life-threatening situations. Although workplace conflict is not life threatening, it feels that way.

In conflict, workers use words rather than lethal weapons to fight. Workers can falsely accuse others, engage in name calling, and hurl slurs and insults; they enlist confederates through social media campaigns, all as a way to intimidate, bully, harass, threaten, dominate, or assault others. Some employees use the courts as a weapon through spurious, malicious lawsuits that are meant to ruin. At its worst, conflict can devolve into literal assault with bodies or weapons.

An individual can flee a conflict by running away literally (calling in sick or hiding in the bathroom) or figuratively (putting off a performance review or feedback on an employee's work). Much of our discussion has been about a figurative running away—avoidance and denial—that many managers engage in when they encounter conflict. Some people may decide that the pain of conflict outweighs the benefits of employment with a team or firm and walk away altogether. If considered with deliberation, this may make sense strategically. Employers can flee conflict by terminating, laying off, or releasing an employee or manager from a contract. When it happens automatically and not strategically, avoiding and denying conflict, it bears repeating, present barriers to effective conflict and dispute resolution. To be effective in conflict or dispute, you need to be present for it with attention, confidence, and balance. Automatically running away undermines your ability to build these muscles so that you can approach conflict with greater skill.

Freezing in response to a threat is another option; a squirrel stops in the middle of the road, or a rabbit, camouflaged to blend in, sits very still for minutes at a time, freezing in response to a threat. In workplace conflict, as Dr. Kenneth Acha, founder of Shaping Destiny, a foundation that serves orphans in Cameroon, Africa, puts it "When people freeze … they don't actively deny it or physically remove themselves from the situation but instead, they disengage, shut up and appease. They simply go along."[1] Strategically, "going along" might be appropriate if your position is wrong or if preserving the relationship has the utmost value. However, chronically and automatically going along may mean you deny your own personal needs to keep the peace and over time can lead to feelings of resentment. Such feelings can undermine effective problem solving.

When we explored the science underlying why pausing is helpful, we began to reveal the biological processes involved in why you may avoid and deny conflict—the fight-flight-freeze response. Looking into the connection between breathing and dealing with fight-flight-freeze will take us a step further toward confidence, balance, and stability in the face of conflict.

What Happens When Threat Happens?

Recall that when individuals perceive a threat, it triggers a complex and well-orchestrated cascade of physiological changes that occur in an instant. In the brain, processes in the amygdala system detect the threat before it registers in your conscious mind and sound a general alarm that signals other systems in the body and brain. The bones release a skeletal hormone called osteocalcin, which triggers the release of adrenaline.[2] Systems in the brain release neurotransmitters and hormones that communicate with the autonomic nervous system. This chain reaction of signals travels through the sympathetic branch of the autonomic nervous system, which prepares the body for fight-flight-freeze. The hormones, called stress hormones, include epinephrine (also known as adrenaline), norepinephrine (also known as noradrenaline), and cortisol; epinephrine and norepinephrine are both hormones and neurotransmitters. The sympathetic nervous system dampens the activity of nonessential physiological processes, like digestion, and signals the circulatory system to divert blood to core organs and muscles in the extremities. Bronchi in the lungs dilate, and breathing quickens to increase the amount of oxygen in the blood. The liver releases stored energy to fuel strength and stamina. With more oxygen and fuel, the heart beats faster—it can feel like it is racing—and blood pressure increases. The pupils dilate so we can see danger better, and other senses are heightened as well. In an instant, the entire body is in a state of high alert, energized and ready to fight, flee, or freeze. All attention is on the threat, real or perceived.

Because surviving the threat is center stage, higher cognitive processes are weaker. Diane Musho Hamilton, a mediator and facilitator, writing in the *Harvard Business Review*, observed, "We can become disoriented in a heated conversation. Complex decision making disappears, as does our access to multiple perspectives. As our attention narrows, we find ourselves trapped in the one perspective that makes us feel the most safe: 'I'm right and you're wrong,' even though we ordinarily see more perspectives."[3]

The neurotransmitters and hormones that circulate during the stress response disrupt memory.[4] You might forget what you planned to say in a meeting with your boss or an argument with a coworker. As Hamilton says, "When our memory is compromised like this, we can't recall something from the past that might help us restore calm. In fact, we can't remember much."[5]

In addition, the physical sensations that accompany the fight-flight-freeze response can be uncomfortable, upsetting, and distracting. Stress hormones may cause trembling or shaking hands or voice. We may sweat and feel that our faces are hot or flushed. Our bodies may feel hot or cold. We'll notice that breathing is rapid and shallow. We may feel that our throat is constricting and notice tension in the body, like clenched hands or jaws. As Hamilton puts it, "We are in the grip of a highly efficient … set of physiological responses. These sensations are not exactly pleasant—they're not meant for relaxation. They're designed to move us to action."[6]

Stanford Professor Robert Sapolsky, a pioneer in the study of the physiological effects of stress on health, emphasizes that the fight-flight-freeze response to life-threatening situations is a survival mechanism in all animals. In the face of genuine threat, it is an asset. For example, according to Sapolsky, it enables a zebra to escape from a lion closing in for the kill. If the zebra survives, it rests for hours to recover. Stores of energy need to be replenished; muscles need to rebuild. If another danger emerges before recovery is complete, the zebra's resources can become depleted.[7]

The fight-flight-freeze response works well for the zebra, as does its camouflage. It worked well for our prehistoric ancestors, who faced similar threats and a lack of safety. It doesn't work well at all for contemporary human beings living in ordinary circumstances. If you are living in a war zone or if your continued survival is threatened by dangers such as famine and disease, activating your stress response is warranted. But for most Westerners, this is not the case. Yet we regularly activate the stress response in response to psychological factors, as if such life-threatening physical stressors existed. This includes how we respond to conflict situations. As Professor Sapolsky observes, when we do this regularly, we have entered the realm of anxiety, neurosis, hostility, and paranoia. And when we do this often enough, we increase our disease risk, because that is not what the stress response evolved for.[8]

The Positive Effects of Controlling the Breath

Controlling the breath is a well-known practice with ancient roots. When I was learning to meditate in India, my yoga teacher first taught me how to control my breath as a way to gain control over my mind and enter meditation itself. Working with the breath is a central feature of yogic practice. Breath control, or pranayama in Sanskrit, has been practiced for thousands of years as a way to enhance or restore health and help gain control over the mind. Contemporary research across a variety of disciplines shows that regulated breathing practices have many benefits, such as reducing symptoms of stress, anxiety, insomnia, post-traumatic stress disorder, and anger, as well as improving emotional control and attention.[9]

Working with the breath is an effective way to calm the nervous system, especially when the stress response is activated. How does slow breathing work? The physiological effects of slow breathing are vast and complex, just like the fight-flight-freeze response. Medical, physiological, and psychological research show that deep breathing affects the cardiovascular system, the brain, digestion, the immune system, and other body systems—the same systems that prepare the body to deal with threat. Earlier, we pointed out that the fight-flight-freeze hormones and neurotransmitters convey information throughout the body through the sympathetic branch of the ANS. The path for deep breathing's effects is also through the autonomic nervous system. The other branch of the ANS is the parasympathetic system. Sometimes, the sympathetic system is called the fight-flight-freeze system. Another name for the parasympathetic system is the rest-and-digest system.

The functions connected to the ANS, such as respiration, heart rate, blood pressure, digestion, and so on, are all involuntary; they happen automatically. However, breathing is an exception: it happens both automatically and under conscious control. And conscious breathing gives us the ability to affect many involuntary processes.

By using our breath consciously, we actively engage the parasympathetic nervous system. In turn, the parasympathetic system calms the body, even when we are in a fight-flight-freeze response, with its consequent physiological changes. When we consciously control the rate, rhythm, and depth of breathing, we increase parasympathetic nervous system activity, return the body to a balanced state, and reduce stress.

When we consciously control the rate, rhythm, and depth of breathing, we increase parasympathetic nervous system activity, return the body to a balanced state, and reduce stress.

In the late 1960s, Dr. Herbert Benson documented the effects of deep, controlled breathing on heart rate, blood pressure, effectiveness of respiration, and other body systems. Participants in his research on stress included a group of people actively practicing meditation. Eventually Benson coined the term "relaxation response" to describe what he learned. But in a 2019 interview with *BrainWorld*, Benson said, "I recognized that we had discovered nothing new because people had been practicing RR techniques for millennia."[10]

Part of the reason slow breathing affects so many other bodily systems has to do with its ability to activate the vagus nerve. The vagus nerve, one of the cranial nerves, begins in the brain stem, ends in the abdomen, and interacts with the heart, lungs, and abdominal organs, including the digestive tract. It is the main pathway of the parasympathetic nervous system and conveys information from the internal organs to the brain and from the brain to the organs.

Vagus nerve activation is an easy-to-access strategy for calming the body.[11] And what is an effective way to activate the vagus nerve? According to research, effective ways involve deep breathing and long exhalations. Some experts describe the vagus nerve as putting the brakes on a revved-up car speeding down the stress-response highway. It reverses the effects that the fight-flight-freeze response triggers, clearing the hormones and neurotransmitters from the cells and bloodstream.

When we were delivered from our mother's womb, we arrived instinctively knowing how to breathe in this deeply life-sustaining way. The challenges of simply making our way in our fast-paced and complex world have contributed to our disconnection from this primal knowledge. With commitment and a willingness to practice, we can reclaim this fundamental intelligence. The following section will help you relearn the skill of deep, life-sustaining breathing and provide suggestions for when and how to practice.

Learning and Strengthening Breathing Practices

There are many breathing practices and exercises. For example, there is diaphragm breathing, alternate nostril breathing (*nadi shodhana*), bellows breathing (*bhastrika*), cleansing breath (*kapalabhati*), ocean breathing (*ujjayi*), counting the breath, holding the breath intermittently, and equal breathing (*sama vritti*), among others—it's a long list.

And there is the mindful attention to natural breathing that we've used in the preceding chapters. Why there are so many different breathing exercises is similar to why there are so many other types of physical exercises. Consider the number of ways to train a bicep muscle—for example, the dumbbell curl, hammer curl, chin up, and so on.

Here, I offer two techniques: forceful breathing and balanced breathing. Both techniques are simple and mobile. The first is a strong intervention for quick relief. This technique helps to quickly calm yourself when you are about to engage in a stressful event, you don't have much time to prepare the mind and body, and the person contributing to your stress is not in front of you. You can also use this exercise as a preliminary exercise before engaging in the balanced breathing practice described later.

The second technique is a deep breathing practice that uses inhalations and exhalations of equal length, duration, and effort from the diaphragm. Some people call this technique coherent breathing. In Sanskrit, this ancient practice is called sama vritti breathing, which means even, regulated breathing.

In the heat of conflict and in the presence of others, most of us would consider it impolite to take a conspicuous, deep breath to calm ourselves. It would visibly signal to the other person that we regard them as a source of distress. However, balanced breathing is inaudible and invisible. We know we are breathing deeply, but those around us don't have to.

Brief, Forceful Breathing Exercise in Preparation for Conflict

Take a comfortable meditation seat with a straight spine and relaxed body, as described in previous chapters. Read the following instructions completely before you try the exercise.

No timer is necessary for this exercise. You'll complete at least three rounds of forceful breathing, more if you like.

For a few moments, bring awareness to your breathing, initially paying attention to its quality without trying to manipulate it in any way. How is your breath now? Is it smooth or choppy? Shallow or deep? Short or long? Just see what is there without creating a story about what's going on.

Next, forcefully from the belly draw in a deep breath through the nostrils. Then forcefully exhale through the nose. It is okay to make a sound as you forcefully exhale. In fact, this is encouraged to promote relaxation. Repeat at least two more times.

Now return to regular breathing for as long as you like. When you're ready, ease out of the practice altogether by slowly bringing awareness back to your surroundings and letting go of this exercise completely.

 ## REFLECTION QUESTIONS

Is this a practice you can use in your everyday life? If so, in a few words describe how or when you could incorporate this practice.

I can use forceful breathing when

_____

_____

_____

_____

If you believe this is not a practice for you, describe why not.

_____

_____

_____

_____

I don't think forceful breathing is a practice I can use in my life because

_____

_____

_____

_____

Balanced Breathing Exercise in Preparation for Conflict

Balanced breathing is one of my favorite breathing techniques. I regularly use this technique while lying in bed before I go to sleep. With each deep exhalation, I am able to release and let go a little bit more of the stressors and cares of the day. With each inhalation, I am able to invite in a little more peace and calm. I feel noticeably more refreshed and grounded the next morning. Feel free to try it yourself before bedtime. Just let yourself go. Don't worry if you're doing it right or for how long you should do it. Let the breath relax you, providing a soothing entryway to sleep.

In balanced breathing, you breathe solely through the nose and breathe deeply from the belly. Practice as if you were in a library, church, or some other sacred space where maintaining discretion is vitally important. We practice subtly because our goal is to use the skill subtly when others are near or when we are in public.

With belly breathing—diaphragmatic or abdominal breathing— we seek to engage the diaphragm by expanding it and engage the chest less or not at all. Recall from the beginning of the chapter that the diaphragm is the respiratory muscle that sits beneath the lungs and in front of the abdominal organs. It separates the thoracic cavity of the torso from the abdominal cavity and is attached to the lower ribs, lower sternum, and the spine in the lower back.

When you are practicing alone, you can use this anatomy lesson to connect with the action of breathing. If you place one hand on the upper abdomen, you can feel the diaphragm move out during inhalations.

The lower rib cage also expands when you inhale. To connect with this sensation, place your hands along each side of the lower rib cage. With correct diaphragmatic breathing, you should notice the rib cage expanding outward.

During this exercise, your attention is partially on counting and partially on watching the expansion of the belly or rib cage (choose one) as you inhale and exhale.

Choose only one point of focus during a practice session. Do not alternate between them during a practice session, as doing so encourages distraction. Leave your hands in place for as long as you like or until you feel comfortable that you are performing the technique correctly.

Take your meditation seat, as described in previous chapters. Read the instructions completely before you begin.

No timer is necessary for this exercise.

Bring awareness to your breathing, initially paying attention to its quality without trying to manipulate it in any way. How is your breath? Is it soft or rough? Constricted or free flowing? Full or shallow? Fleeting or enduring? Just try to notice what is there without judging whether your breath is good or bad.

In balanced breathing, we are trying to maintain uniformity of the inhalations and exhalations. Each should be of equal duration and effort. Take a deep inhalation through the nose to the count of four: one, two, three, four. Then exhale through the nose to the count of four: one, two, three, four. It doesn't matter if your count is fast or slow as long as you count at the same pace for inhalations and exhalations.

Again, draw in a deep breath through the nostrils to the count of four. Notice the slight pause at the top of the breath. Now exhale through the nostrils to the count of four. Notice the slight pause at the bottom of the breath. Notice the expansion and contraction of the belly or rib cage.

If at any time feelings of anxiety or stress rise to the level of distress, or you find that counting to four is unmanageable for whatever reason, you have options. You can alter the count, always making sure the exhalation and the inhalation are the same length. Or you can release the exercise and return to a grounded space, such as simple breath awareness. You can even open your eyes to reorient and ground yourself.

Stay with this practice for as long as you like and can do so comfortably, without tension or distress. Then, take a few moments to ease out of the practice. If your eyes were partially or completely closed, slowly lift your eyelids. Notice what you see. Then begin to expand your awareness outward from narrow to wide. Show appreciation to yourself for making the effort to develop yourself. Then, see what part of the practice you can carry with you in your next endeavor or task.

REFLECTION QUESTIONS

How does your body feel now?
I noticed my body feels like

_____

_____

_____

_____

What different sensations do you notice?
I noticed my sensations include

_____

_____

_____

_____

How does your mind feel?
My mind feels

_____

_____

_____

_____

What differences in your thoughts or feeling of mental readiness do
you notice?
I notice my thoughts and feelings of mental readiness are now

_____

_____

_____

_____

What shifts in your emotions do you notice?

I notice my emotions are

_____

_____

_____

_____

WORKING WITH CHALLENGES DURING BREATHING PRACTICE SESSIONS

Controlling our breath with intention for an extended time is not how most of us usually breathe. As we sit down to work with breathing practices, if we feel particularly anxious or stressed, it may take time to corral the breath in a smooth and methodical way. Controlling the breath can be even more challenging when practicing under the stress of a conflict visualization situation. To corral the breath, you can pair audible, forceful breathing with balanced breathing in one session. Forceful breathing can help the body calm down more quickly, and you can then more readily engage with coherent, or sama vritti, breathing.

During any session, smooth, synchronized breathing may never happen, and that's all right. As with mindfulness practice, let go of what you think should happen, and let whatever arises arise. Regardless of how easy or difficult it is to practice, we are gaining insight into the relationship between breath and mind, and this alone is useful information. Try to exercise patience and care. Start wherever you are. We are building new muscles, and there may be discomfort, restlessness, or anxiousness as you work with these practices, and that's okay. Let it be.

Breathing Leads to Wise Action

When you are in the heat of conflict, you can draw on all of the learning and training you've accomplished thus far, combined with the breath, to help you immediately shift your physiology to a calmer state. This will provide you space to make wiser choices, as we'll discuss in the next chapter.

Start wherever you are. We are building new muscles, and there may be discomfort, restlessness, or anxiousness as you work with these practices, and that's okay. Let it be.

To prepare for choosing wise action, first practice SNAP. Bring awareness (See It) to the thoughts, feelings, and sensations you are having in your body and mind as the conflict arises. Then, name (Name It) what you are experiencing—for example, stress, anxiety, fear, or anger. Then, accept (Accept It) that this is the current state of affairs, even though you may not like it.

Then Pause and Breathe to calm your body and mind so that you can better prepare for wise action. Activate the breath intentionally. Use balanced breathing by consciously bringing your awareness to your belly and breathing deeply from the belly and through the nose. Continue pausing and breathing for however long you find it helpful.

Many people find that pausing and accessing the breath creates the mental space to be more reflective, which increases the chances of making wiser decisions.

In conflict and with calm awareness, reflect on what you want to do now. How do you choose wise action under the stressful conditions of conflict?

CHAPTER SEVEN

Choose It

Everything can be taken from a [person] but one thing:
the last of the human freedoms—to choose one's attitude in
any given set of circumstances, to choose one's own way.

—VIKTOR FRANKL, PSYCHIATRIST,
AUTHOR, HOLOCAUST SURVIVOR

W hile writing this book, I invited colleagues to share their stories about the impact meditation has in their lives. Here is one of them.

I've tried for many years to establish a consistent meditation practice and have failed at each attempt. Time constraints, life, stress, other things to do—you name it—all got in the way. Meditation just didn't happen. Then about two and a half years ago, I reached a crisis point in my job. I'm a retired air force attorney who now works for the air force as a civilian attorney in fiscal law and federal ethics law. Extremely dissatisfied with my situation, I began to think seriously (or at least daydream) about quitting on the spot and telling the hypocritical "leaders" surrounding me exactly what I thought of them. This dissatisfaction went on for quite a while, and it had a negative effect on all aspects of my life.

In time, I took a vacation and tried to sort things out. I spent a lot of time in thought and prayer and got advice from trusted friends. This led me to the conclusion that since I was very close to being eligible for a second retirement, which I very much wanted, I needed to find a way to deal productively with my situation without having a stress breakdown or saying something that would get me fired. I was inspired to write a list of how I should be acting and how I should be dealing with my job. It was a reality list, not a too-high-expectations list. I typed it as a bulleted list and taped it on the office wall next to my computer.

Now, every morning when I get to work, before I do anything else, I read that list as a way to reset my expectations for my day and myself. Then I kneel and say a short prayer of thanks for my job, which really is a good job and takes care of my family very well. Reset and gratitude. Throughout the day, I find myself glancing at the list to remind myself, for instance, that certain things are just not my problem and to just let them go.

This practice, call it what you may, saved me. I've rarely missed a day of this practice since I hung up my list two and a half years ago. It has brought me peace of mind and spirit and the ability to deal with what I need to deal with and leave the rest alone. It has lowered my stress level greatly and enabled me to enjoy my job again and be a better person at home. I'm now six months from retirement and have no doubt about making it to the finish line.

When you asked me whether I have a meditation practice, my first answer was, "I don't really have a practice; I don't meditate." Then I glanced over at my list and thought, "But I practice every day. Maybe that counts and could be useful to people like me who find a formal meditation practice challenging."

Choosing wise action in the face of conflict seems like a goal that is out of most people's reach, like the "too-high-expectations list." But my colleague's experience shows that insight, reflection, and pausing open the door to wisdom, even without a formal mindfulness meditation practice. Wise action and wisdom may only be a matter of taking the time and making the space to become aware of your values and align your behavior with them.

In Chapter 6, we learned that working with our breath in a deliberate and controlled way alters our physiology and creates cognitive and emotional space for us to operate in. Something as simple as taking three deep inhalations and exhalations during conflict can create that space. And we can take these breaths in a way that looks natural and does not draw undue attention to oneself or the situation.

The last step in the SNAP BC method is choosing a course of action to take. Make no mistake: we have choices about how we respond in the face of conflict. But in the heat of the moment,

> *Make no mistake: we have choices about how we respond in the face of conflict.*

choice does not appear to be an option; what to do seems somehow out of reach or inapparent. In the middle of the storm of conflict, it feels like our minds, emotions, and behaviors possess us or control us. When we are not mindful in conflict, it appears to ourselves that we are not in control.

Being human and subject to the biological processes that entails, like the fight-flight-freeze response and the relaxation response, our first reaction may always be that feeling of not being in control or having no choices. SNAP BC's response to this fundamental human condition is to build our capacity for standing in the storm of conflict with greater resilience and wisdom, to build our ability to just be with whatever arises, without running away, denying, or rejecting it—that is, to stand in conflict with courage.

Why Wisdom Matters and Why Its Absence Is a Problem

Wisdom matters because it enables us to distinguish between beneficial and detrimental actions and guides us toward skillful actions that have a chance of producing constructive results. When we use wisdom to guide our actions, we acknowledge that we should strive to perform skillful, beneficial actions and abandon their opposite. Moreover, with wisdom, we recognize that negative consequences exist for unwise or foolish action.

In conflict, leaders face choices to act with courage or fear, humility or arrogance, understanding or presupposition, self-awareness or egotism, and insight or ignorance. Wisdom, with its grounding in insight and self-awareness, sets the stage for making these choices.

Acting with wisdom can create the opportunity to gain others' respect, bring out their best behavior, and inspire them to follow your actions. On the other hand, when we act foolishly, rashly, or reactively, we can undermine our own integrity and, in the process, generate a loss of trust and confidence among the people we report to, peers, and the people who report to us.

One form of reactive behavior that undermines trust is seeking revenge in the form of retaliation when an employee reports wrongdoing. Employers face one of their most significant legal challenges when managers retaliate against employees who have sought to blow the whistle on what they perceive as unlawful behavior or protect themselves by filing complaints. Retaliation is the most often filed discrimination complaint (53.8 percent in 2019[1]) and has the highest success rate of any type of discrimination claim from the employee's point of view. There are currently more retaliation cases than sexual discrimination and sexual harassment cases, despite the #MeToo movement.

In my experience as a labor and employment lawyer, while many managers understand the legal prohibition against punishing someone for pursuing their rights, many struggle with the notion that they should treat someone who has lodged a damning, threatening, existentially undermining complaint the same as a model employee. Managers can have strong negative emotions toward an individual who makes claims that seriously threaten their reputation and position. Making the situation more volatile, most employees filing such claims continue to work for their bosses. How can people work together effectively under such circumstances?

The mere allegation of retaliation very effectively fosters animosity and destroys trust with those below and above you. It sends a message that you will not tolerate those who challenge you or welcome them as part of your team.

Defending retaliation complaints can cost a company hundreds of thousands of dollars in legal fees. And a judgment or finding of retaliation can mean paying the winning party's attorney fees and costs, a loss of reputation to the organization, and possible disciplinary action against the offending manager—all because the manager could not effectively navigate the strong emotions rising from the conflict between an employee pursuing their rights and their own sense of self.

Some years ago, I was the legal advisor for labor and employment matters at a federal government agency. A complex case of retaliation at the agency illustrates the destructive consequences of reactive choices. The case included sexual harassment, elements of whistleblowing, and gender bias. It began when Cathy filed a complaint that she had been sexually harassed by her manager, Kevin. The complaint triggered an investigation during which Cathy's coworkers were interviewed.

One coworker, Theresa, was a talented employee whom the agency head planned to reward with a promotion and transfer to a more desirable location. Cathy filed her complaint, and the investigation began around the time Theresa was to transfer to her new position. During her interview, the internal affairs investigator asked Theresa whether Kevin had sexually harassed her, as others alleged he had done to them. Because Kevin had threatened to harm Theresa and her family if she revealed his despicable behavior, Theresa falsely denied that Kevin had also sexually harassed her.

The investigator questioned other witnesses and gathered more information. As sometimes happens in such investigations, the investigator interviewed Theresa, along with other witnesses, a second time. This time Theresa confessed that Kevin had forced her to perform sex acts upon him in his office and to keep quiet about it, under threat of termination and harm to her family. Judging the threat to be credible, Theresa complied.

Theresa's initial false statement left her in a vulnerable position. Federal agencies have a policy that requires employees to respond truthfully and completely when answering investigators' questions. No one doubted Theresa's story that Kevin had sexually assaulted and threatened her. However, Theresa had to think about the consequences of telling the truth. Would Kevin carry out his threat? Would her promotion be jeopardized? Yet Theresa had not initially told the truth, as required by agency policy.

The unit's leader, Rick, had to respond to Theresa's violation of policy. He had any number of responses at his disposal. He could show wisdom and compassion toward Theresa by reassuring her that her job and promotion were safe, expressing regret and sympathy for what happened to her, or assuring her that justice would be done, and no retribution would occur. Had he done any of those things, Rick would have shown his employees and managers what wise leadership looks like.

However, Rick did none of them. Instead, he chose a less courageous, unwise path and pursued a course of action that rested on a technicality to Theresa's detriment. He sought to rescind Theresa's promotion on the grounds that she had violated the agency's policy. Moreover, Rick sought to discipline Theresa for "lying during an official investigation."

Rick's actions put the agency at great legal risk, prompted an investigation by an outside agency, and harmed the positive reputation the agency had worked hard to earn. His choice was unwise, perhaps even foolish, given the potential consequences, and it jeopardized his relationships with his team, peers, and subordinates. He undermined the respect other colleagues and team members held for him and inspired them to question his ability to lead wisely.

Why Rick chose retaliation as his response is less important than what he could have done differently. The SNAP BC method offers us the chance to develop alternatives. We can use it to interrupt a retaliatory response—or any other negative response—to a perceived threat to our integrity and choose something different. It enables us to recognize that we have agency, even in difficult circumstances. By practicing SNAP BC, we decrease our chances of being reactive and increase our chances of choosing wise actions.

> *The SNAP BC method offers us the chance to develop alternatives. We can use it to interrupt a retaliatory response—or any other negative response—to a perceived threat to our integrity and choose something different. It enables us to recognize that we have agency, even in difficult circumstances.*

Throughout the book, I've described the alternative to negative responses during conflict as wise action. But this begs the question: What is wisdom?

What Is Wisdom?

We all have the capacity to act with wisdom in the moment. It is not an attribute reserved for a select few. Nor is it an ideal or merely something we know when we see it. Wisdom is a form of advanced cognitive and emotional development that we gain from experiences rather than from reading lots of books or having expert knowledge about a subject.

Monika Ardelt, a sociology professor at the University of Florida who studies wisdom, and her colleagues consulted with wisdom experts from around the world to build a definition of the concept. The experts describe three dimensions of wisdom: cognitive, reflective, and affective.[2]

- Cognitive aspects of wisdom relate to how we think about life and events. Understanding that all human beings share essential positive and negative qualities and that we must make decisions in the face of uncertainty is a hallmark of wise thinking.

- Reflective aspects of wisdom relate to how we perceive life and our relationship to it. Being able to look at the world from different points of view and know that others are not responsible for how we feel or the situation we are in is fundamental to wise reflection. Self-examination, self-awareness, and self-insight are also fundamental qualities of wisdom.

- Affective aspects of wisdom describe how we relate to life emotionally. When we are emotionally wise, we respond to adversity with resilience and engage with others in positive ways rather than with negativity or indifference. Emotional regulation and sympathy, kindness, care, and concern for others—that is, compassionate love—are equally important affective aspects of wisdom.

These characteristics of wisdom might sound familiar. The mindfulness exercises we have been working with develop our capacity for awareness of what we think, feel, and sense in the moment. The practice is reflective, develops insight into the qualities and experiences that all human beings share, and builds emotional regulation. These characteristics underpin what many experts say are the three most important components of wise leadership: having a sense of self-awareness and emotional intelligence, knowing what to do, and acting with the greater good in mind.[3]

How SNAP BC Cultivates Wisdom

As I pointed out in earlier chapters, many managers cut themselves off from taking wise action, at least in the short run, by avoiding conflict. Underlying the many ways to avoid conflict—for example, delaying performance discussions or not taking corrective or disciplinary action—is a manager's fear that he or she might not have the internal resources to confront the situation. However, avoiding conflict is unwise. It encourages small problems to blossom into big troubles. It also has a negative impact on teams: one person's workload can increase when a coworker's performance is poor; morale decreases when employees see their peers engage in misconduct without consequence; bad behavior that goes unchecked lowers standards and emboldens staff to not give their best efforts. We know that avoiding problems like these is more important than avoiding conflict.

The SNAP BC approach helps you shift your behavior away from avoiding conflict and taking unwise actions in general. Each step fosters wise action because it helps cultivate the cognitive, affective, and reflective dimensions of wisdom, as described above.

Cognitive aspects of wisdom. SNAP BC addresses how we think about circumstances related to conflict. It offers a framework for methodically and nonjudgmentally observing our thinking and how it influences the way we respond to conflict and others involved in it.

Affective aspects of wisdom. The Naming and Acceptance steps of SNAP BC help us see how we relate to conflict emotionally. These steps develop our capacity to relate to our emotional states with objectivity and compassion rather than by suppressing or avoiding them. By compassionately observing and accepting difficult emotions, the SNAP BC approach helps us build emotional resilience in the face of adversity.

Reflective aspects of wisdom. At the heart of SNAP BC are mindfulness practices that cultivate awareness. Mindfulness develops our awareness of what is happening in our lives and our relationship to our lives. It fosters self-awareness and insight. By paying attention to each moment, we develop awareness of conflict as it emerges. This awareness enables us to take a reflective stance toward the role we and others play in conflict.

These characteristics of wisdom might sound familiar. The mindfulness exercises we have been working with develop our capacity for awareness of what we think, feel, and sense in the moment. The practice is reflective, develops insight into the qualities and experiences that all human beings share, and builds emotional regulation. These characteristics underpin what many experts say are the three most important components of wise leadership: having a sense of self-awareness and emotional intelligence, knowing what to do, and acting with the greater good in mind.[3]

The hallmarks of wisdom are understanding that all human beings share wholesome and unwholesome qualities, that life is uncertain, that we are responsible for how we feel and what we choose, and that compassion and resilience serve us best, regardless of circumstances. Practicing the SNAP BC approach creates an environment that enhances our capacity to gain these insights and helps foster those wisdom qualities.

SNAP BC teaches how to cultivate a state of mind that is objective, nonjudgmental, and compassionate, one that doesn't take everything personally. Through the steps See It, Name It, and Accept It, we learn to see how things operate in the world without that seeing being so colored by our wishes, hopes, and biases. With this more dispassionate point of view, we begin to generate an emotional fierceness. Our understanding is not so "me," "my," or "I" focused, and our tight grip on how we want things to be loosens. As this happens, we open up and take in the perspectives of others.

This dispassionate state of mind creates a reflective mental space between what we perceive and how we respond. In that space is the opportunity for greater insight. And that insight increases the chances for more thoughtful decision making and greater compassion for others and ourselves. By developing and supporting this mindset, SNAP BC creates the necessary conditions for wisdom.

What could cultivating a dispassionate state of mind mean in practice? With a little mental space, a manager might lean into, rather than turn away from, difficult conversations with poorly performing employees and do so early.

When you wait until you get the third mistake-filled report from a team member, you might take unwise actions that look like frustration and anger spiking. Underlying the anger might be self-centered thoughts like, "I can't believe this is happening to me again," "I don't deserve this disrespect," or "Why does this always happen to me? I don't see staff doing this to my colleagues. This employee must hate me." The unwise actions might end with storming into the direct report's office, demanding that they fix the mistakes right now, and threatening the employee with consequences like demotion or termination.

Using a SNAP BC response, the manager would become aware of the strong emotion the mistake-filled report elicited and would name it—anger, let's say. The manager would then accept feeling upset in that moment at the consistently poor performance this employee has been delivering. Pausing, the manager would refrain from rash judgments or actions. Then, taking a few deep breaths to calm the fight-flight-freeze response accompanying the anger, they would center and ground themselves. In this expanded mental space, the manager would reach for a more dispassionate approach to the situation.

Working with the SNAP BC method over time, the manager can loosen the tendency to see everything through the "I" lens. She can become less concerned that the report reflects negatively on her personally and what kind of manager this must make her and can increasingly turn her thinking outward, toward the employee, team, and organization. Curious, she can wonder what is going on with the employee such that she's consistently been performing at a subpar level. The manager can consider the results of the poor performance beyond herself. Will it result in increased work for the team? What impact will it have on morale? And how is the subpar performance affecting the company's larger mission and goals?

The manager's increased dispassionate view of the world opens her vision, rather than narrowing it. With a broader view of the issues, she can see and choose from various options: consult with human resources about options regarding the employee's consistently subpar performance; have another employee rework the urgent report; have a formal performance discussion with the employee to ensure the employee understands the job requirements and expectations and determine what the manager can do to help the employee meet these expectations.

The process of seeing our emotions, calming them, pausing, and breathing creates an opportunity to choose a wise course of action. Working with SNAP BC enables us to avoid our habitual, reactive responses, which too often lead us to make unwise, foolish choices.

Earlier, I told the story of a government agency manager, Rick, who unwisely decided to rescind an employee's promotion because she had violated a policy that required employees to respond truthfully and completely when interviewed during an investigation. Rick's actions were bereft of wisdom. Using Professor Ardelt's paradigm, we can see that he did not try to understand the deeper meaning of the employee's failure to be candid during the first interview—recall, it was an investigation of sexual harassment; his choice showed a lack of cognizance. The affective aspect was missing, as the decision to rescind the promotion and consider disciplinary action lacked compassion for the employee's plight. The reflective aspect of wisdom was absent because he chose not to perceive the problem from the employee's perspective. What actions might have unfolded if the manager learned and practiced SNAP BC?

Wisdom Can Be Trained

As we've seen throughout the book, emotions often underpin our habitual reactions to conflict. However, just as we are not at the mercy of our knee-jerk reactions, we are not at the mercy of our emotions, as strong as they may feel in the heat of conflict. We have other options, wiser choices. And we already have the capacity to make those wiser choices. We just need some training in how to do so. In fact, the level of wisdom we possess is not static or unchanging.

Professor Ardelt and other experts agree that wisdom entails cognitive and emotional development that people gain from their life experiences. Wisdom is not an unchanging, immutable quality. Because mindfulness practice helps us pay attention, on purpose, to what we are experiencing in the present moment, and what might be learned from those experiences, it is an exceptional tool for cultivating wisdom and increasing our capacity for wise training.

USING MINDFULNESS TO CULTIVATE WISDOM

The present moment is often messy. Employees refuse to share resources. Employers may get ghosted—a worker simply stops coming to work without notice or explanation. A worker might bully coworkers. Executives want reports and products at the speed of the internet, so managers press their teams to deliver their work as fast as possible. Because of tight deadlines, the work contains errors or other flaws, or teams miss deadlines. Without self-awareness, executives, managers, and team members rely on habitual mindsets and behaviors. In the moment, tempers flare, people may say words they later regret, and conflict ensues.

The SNAP BC method enables us to learn to better stand in all that messiness and do so in a more emotionally grounded, insightful, and calm way. It helps us overcome our tight grip on one perspective, habitual reactions, and tendency to panic when we feel threatened. With mindfulness, we tune into the entirety of our experience, whether frustration, anger, boredom, intrigue, joy, or uncertainty, and hold it in our conscious awareness. This is a huge first step away from unconsciously relating and reacting to the world. When we consider the world from multiple perspectives and face perceived threats with calm, we create a mental space in which we can just be with our experience in the moment.

In his book *Man's Search for Meaning*, the source of this chapter's opening quote, Victor Frankl talked about how we can use this mental space in a positive way. Frankl wrote about his time as a prisoner in a Nazi concentration camp and, reflecting on his experiences, discussed how we can make meaning in our lives even in tragic circumstances. He concluded that when all other freedoms are gone, human beings still have the freedom to choose their attitude, regardless of the circumstances. I would add that recognizing we have the freedom to choose provides the environment for developing wisdom and the opportunity for wise action.

As we've seen throughout the book, emotions often underpin our habitual reactions to conflict. However, just as we are not at the mercy of our knee-jerk reactions, we are not at the mercy of our emotions, as strong as they may feel in the heat of conflict. We have other options, wiser choices. And we already have the capacity to make those wiser choices. We just need some training in how to do so.

If making wiser choices is the goal, it's helpful to have predetermined principles or values to guide decision making. How we respond to others in difficult moments has enduring consequences for others and ourselves. We model behavior for peers and direct reports, set expectations, and make statements in our words and deeds about how we value a relationship. In the space between provocation and response, we make choices that shape us as human beings, shape our future, and shape our relationships to others in the workplace.

What Are Your Personal and Organizational Values, and Why Do They Matter?

On my wall, I keep a list I call the Inspirators, people who display qualities I admire. I respect and want to emulate the fundamental ways they show up in the world. They represent the values that I aspire to embody in my own life and work. I wrote their names and those qualities that resonate with me. On my list is the Dalai Lama, for joyful effort and connection to others. Nelson Mandela is on the list for courage and resilience. The Buddha is there for enlightened action, lovingkindness, compassion, and patience.

Our values are deeply embedded in beliefs about what is important to us, and they are largely outside our conscious awareness. Yet they are a profound force in motivating behavior and influencing the types of decisions we make. Our personal values answer questions such as "What do I think is good, beneficial, wholesome, or important?" Values may include characteristics like hard work, creativity, courage, resilience, compassion, leadership, responsibility, or harmony.

When we act in accordance with our principles and values, then what we say and do makes them real and apparent to everyone, including ourselves. However, most of us don't take the time to articulate and write down our values, even though they motivate so much of our behavior. Nevertheless, when we act in a way that aligns with our values, we have the sense that we are acting in accordance with our highest selves. This internal congruence brings with it a feeling of contentment. We feel uplifted, inspired, and connected.

The sitcom *Frasier* had a great recurring theme about misaligned values. The show was about two highly competitive brothers, both psychiatrists, and their retired police officer dad. The very prim and proper Niles Crane regarded honesty as sacrosanct. Whenever he told a lie, even a small one, before he could intellectualize the situation, his body immediately reacted with a nosebleed. It was a great illustration of how our bodies express the tension that results when we engage in a behavior misaligned with our values.

An Exercise to Uncover Your Personal Values

As you prepare to choose a course of action for addressing conflict, it's helpful to have a guiding light. This North Star will help guide your actions and help you check whether the way you are responding to conflict aligns with your values. A simple and effective way for uncovering your values is to make your own list of Inspirators.

Right now, pause. Take a few minutes to reflect on your heroes, those who inspire you. What qualities do they demonstrate that you connect with, that you aspire to embody? In the space below, write the name of one to three Inspirators and a few of their qualities that inspire you.

My Inspirator's Name:

What I admire:

_____

_____

_____

_____

My Inspirator's Name:
What I admire:

_____

_____

_____

_____

My Inspirator's Name:
What I admire:

_____

_____

_____

_____

As you prepare to choose a course of action for resolving conflict, check inside yourself. Ask, "How can my words and behavior align with what I value?" When harmony is the value, for example, aligned behavior may mean using words that signal shared circumstance, remind what has been overcome in the past, and express confidence that this challenge, too, will be met. Words misaligned with harmony would draw distinctions or separate you from your counterpart. Expressing harmony may mean arranging to have the conversation in a private place or in surroundings where power dynamics are not used as leverage.

An Exercise to Uncover Your Organization's Values

Organizational values may include characteristics like integrity, honesty, excellence, compassion, and accountability—the list is practically endless. Many organizations spend countless hours toiling over and wordsmithing values statements that you see on plaques hanging in the cafeteria or meeting rooms or included in email signature lines. My observation from working with teams is that putting their values, which are ordinarily invisible, opaque, or unthought of, into words is a clarifying experience. At some level, the effort to clarify what the organization cares about and what it prioritizes adds value. Putting values into words can be revelatory and may prompt some serious soul searching.

Pause again. Now consider your organization's heroes. Who does your organization consider its heroes? The people might be readily apparent in things like your organization's origin story, leaders' public statements, TED Talks, or marketing campaigns. Finding your organization's heroes may involve a bit more sleuthing, in which case you should feel free to ask colleagues. In the space below, write the names of one to three organizational heroes and a few of each one's qualities.

My organization's hero:

What my organization admires:

_____

_____

_____

_____

My organization's hero:

What my organization admires:

_____

_____

_____

_____

My organization's hero:

What my organization admires:

_____

_____

_____

_____

Notice the extent of overlap or gaps between your individual values and those of the organization.

As you know, organizations don't manifest values; people do. No amount of artful drafting can replace the experience of living your or your organization's values in day-to-day workplace interactions. If you learned after the preceding exercise that your personal values align with those of your organization, you are likely to find more organizational support for the conflict resolution strategies you adopt, whether those are taking care of employees, honesty, transparency, respect for people, professionalism, or whatever they may be.

However, if there are significant gaps between your personal values and those of the organization, it will be more difficult for you to align your conflict resolution strategies and behaviors with the values the organization says it cares about. This misalignment may present an opportunity for you to start a dialogue to explore these gaps with the aim of bringing the organization's expressed values and yours into greater alignment in the context of conflict resolution.

As you prepare to choose a course of action for resolving conflict, check inside yourself. Ask, "How can my words and behavior align with organizational values?" Where honesty and transparency are highly valued, this might mean, for example, talking about your doubts, misgivings, or biases—mind states that are not visible to your counterpart in a conflict, but which may contribute to the conflict. If respect for people is prized, this might mean intentionally behaving in ways that say, "I hear you." This respect could include deep listening skills—for example, maintaining eye contact, avoiding distractions (don't return emails or texts while talking, and turn off the phone), showing curiosity, and asking questions.

Preparation for Conflict

Understanding your values underpins and supports what skill or technique you intend to deploy in a situation. Many techniques have the potential to be useful in conversations with those we're in conflict with. These techniques include asking thoughtful questions, framing the conversation, and finding common ground. Deep listening is an exceptional tool to deploy in conflict situations. But if you lack respect for the person in front of you, your ability to integrate and embody deep listening, for example, or any other technique will be much less effective. In other words, whatever technique you use must align with your underlying values. When you understand what you and your organization value, you will have a greater ability to effectively use techniques that help to defuse and calm conflict.

The point here is that it is advisable to think about your values and consider how you can align skillful decision making in conflict with them. I regularly review my Inspirators list to stay connected to my higher self and the values I'd like to bring to all aspects of my work and personal life. The air force attorney's opening story presented another version of this. Recall that he wrote a list of ways he wanted to act so that he could maintain a productive outlook while performing a job he needed but wasn't thrilled about. Each morning he consulted that list, and this reset his expectations. When you make yourself consciously aware of your principles and values, you enable yourself to plan how to use them in advance. In the emotionally charged situation of conflict, being able to draw on value-based behaviors helps short circuit the tendency to rely on habitual responses.

I suggested before that if making wiser choices is the goal, having principles or values that you've previously considered and adopted— your North Star—is valuable to guide decision making. Now that you have identified your values, you are in a position to see how those values influence how you can respond to conflict with greater wisdom. The following exercise helps you prepare to address conflict by identifying those values you want to draw on and align with when addressing conflict. To help you decide which of those values might be appropriate to consider for this purpose, recall the discussion that acting with wisdom entails cognitive, reflective, and affective components. So, for example, drawing upon my own list of Inspirators, and acknowledging the three domains of wisdom, when I address conflict, I want my words and actions to be in service of the values of:

1. Openness and creativity (cognitive)

2. Ability to take the other's perspective and show compassion (reflective)

3. Loving kindness and patience (affective)

Take a moment, right now, to pause and reflect on how you can employ your values, infused with wisdom, when dealing with conflict. Write your responses below.

When addressing conflict, I want my words and action to be in service of the values of:

1. (cognitive) _____

2. (reflective) _____

3. (affective) _____

You may consider posting your list in a place where you can see it every day to remind yourself of your greatest aspirational values when it comes to handling conflict. If you have a contemplative practice (meditation, prayer, or journaling, for example) or are considering initiating one, I invite you to consider incorporating the insights you've gained from these exercises into your practice to deepen and integrate them. For example, you can visualize yourself responding to conflict by saying and doing things that align with your value of building connection, if that is a value on your list. Or in your journaling, you might reflect on and write about the benefits to you and your team from behaving in value-based ways, as well as the disadvantages when you don't. Reflecting on the benefits is important because it keeps you connected to your why. By frequently reminding yourself of your aspirations and their benefits, you increasingly integrate them so that they become your new way of being. You are building a new habit, which prepares you for engaging in the actual experience of conflict in a new, more constructive way.

Bringing Wisdom to Your Response in the Heat of Conflict

Aligning your actions with your values is a deeply personal undertaking. In addition, the results of alignment may look different for different conflicts because each conflict and the people involved are unique. However, the following checklist can guide the process of aligning your actions with your values as conflict arises.

Step 1. Check inside yourself. Using what you have learned in the SNAP BC approach, check:

- What is happening in my internal landscape? What am I thinking? What emotions am I feeling? What sensations am I experiencing in my body?

- What do my thoughts, emotions, and sensations mean? For example, in some people a churning stomach may signal fear and nervousness.

Step 2. Check outside yourself.
- Pick the right time. What time will be conducive to you and the other person addressing the situation with greater calm and presence?

- Choose the right place. What place will honor respect and privacy for you, your counterpart, and your larger work team?

Step 3. Align your approach with your values.
- Consider your highest values. What values that you uncovered and articulated in the preceding exercises do you want to bring to the conversation? These values could be attributes like compassion, harmony, accountability, responsibility, presence, and attunement.

- What approach or strategy would best align with those values? These could be mindful or deep listening, taking the other's perspective, or accepting having to make difficult decisions.

CHAPTER EIGHT

Conclusion– Walking the Path

It is important to expect nothing, to take every experience, including the negative ones, as merely steps on the path, and to proceed.

—RAM DASS, SPIRITUAL TEACHER, PSYCHOLOGIST, AUTHOR

W orkplace conflict will be with us as long as there are places where the rich diversity of humanity come together to work toward a common aim. Unfortunately, in conflict, too many managers lead from a place of habit and fear, where reactive conflict decisions lead to destructive organizational outcomes, the Before paradigm.

Managing the Self in Conflict— BEFORE

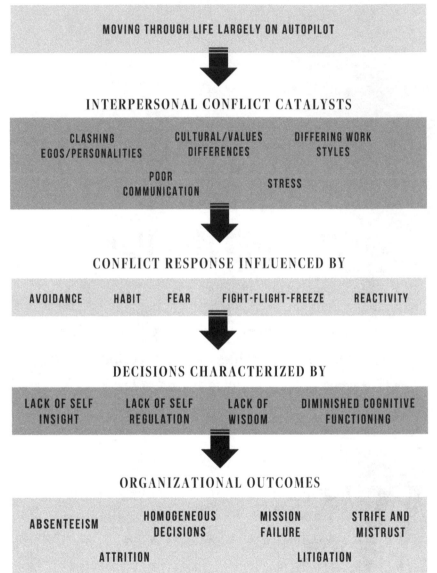

PREPARATION

MOVING THROUGH LIFE LARGELY ON AUTOPILOT

INTERPERSONAL CONFLICT CATALYSTS

CLASHING EGOS/PERSONALITIES   CULTURAL/VALUES DIFFERENCES   DIFFERING WORK STYLES

POOR COMMUNICATION   STRESS

CONFLICT RESPONSE INFLUENCED BY

AVOIDANCE   HABIT   FEAR   FIGHT-FLIGHT-FREEZE   REACTIVITY

DECISIONS CHARACTERIZED BY

LACK OF SELF INSIGHT   LACK OF SELF REGULATION   LACK OF WISDOM   DIMINISHED COGNITIVE FUNCTIONING

ORGANIZATIONAL OUTCOMES

ABSENTEEISM   HOMOGENEOUS DECISIONS   MISSION FAILURE   STRIFE AND MISTRUST

ATTRITION   LITIGATION

Yet each conflict offers the opportunity to show leadership. Whether you are involved in a conflict, someone asks you for advice on how to resolve a conflict, or you coach others on conflict resolution, you have regular, ongoing opportunities to build capacity for effectively handling conflict. While some leaders and managers consider this a curse, others see it as a gift. However, the problem is not so much with the fact of conflict—that conflict exists. Rather, the problem lies in how we respond to it.

The most popular method of addressing conflict is nonstrategic avoidance—that is, avoiding conflict out of habit, rather than as a strategic decision formed after deliberate consideration. We avoid conflict because otherwise, we might demonstrate incompetence or a lack of being in command or control. We might appear weak or unknowledgeable. Our automatic response to these feelings about conflict is a product of years of conditioning.

However, conflict doesn't magically disappear simply because we avoid it. Nonstrategic avoidance can be an unsatisfactory, unhelpful response. Moreover, by avoiding conflict, managers give up the opportunity to develop resilience, to train, develop, and strengthen their capacity to meet conflict skillfully—that is, with wisdom and compassion.

Thus, while it might not seem like it, conflict offers a gift: the opportunity to develop our fortitude and capacity to be in conflict with courage, skillfulness, and wisdom. In conflict, emotions run high, largely because the chance of losing face is great. The skills—emotional intelligence skills—that help us navigate conflict are the capacity to see what is happening within ourselves and then manage our emotions. However, few people are taught these skills growing up, and conflict management training often doesn't address how to develop these skills. Many people understand and accept the importance of high emotional intelligence, but we have no road map for how to apply emotional intelligence during conflict.

To develop the skills to manage ourselves in conflict requires turning the lens away from conflict and toward ourselves, endeavoring to generate self-awareness and insight. Why? When we turn inward to find answers, relying less on external sources, we tap into the deep well of wisdom that's within us.

Although each of us has wisdom that we accumulate from experience, we also have habitual ways of being in the world that block our access to that wisdom. I developed SNAP BC as a systematic approach to dislodge those blocks, gain access to wisdom, and engage with conflict with strength, courage, and resilience.

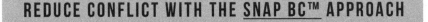

REDUCE CONFLICT WITH THE SNAP BC™ APPROACH

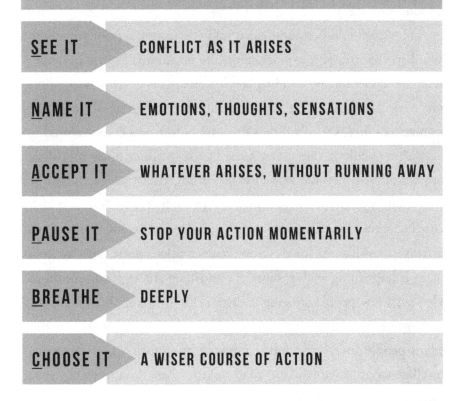

SEE IT — CONFLICT AS IT ARISES

NAME IT — EMOTIONS, THOUGHTS, SENSATIONS

ACCEPT IT — WHATEVER ARISES, WITHOUT RUNNING AWAY

PAUSE IT — STOP YOUR ACTION MOMENTARILY

BREATHE — DEEPLY

CHOOSE IT — A WISER COURSE OF ACTION

This book is an instruction manual for developing and training our minds and bodies for more skillful action in conflict. Mindfulness practice underpins the approach.

We prepare the ground by increasing our awareness more generally. Since we habitually live on autopilot—our attention captured by thoughts about the past and the future, or by a constant stream of thoughts—the first step is to wake up to what is happening in our lives. When we do so, we may notice that what we observe is uncomfortable or even disturbing. It is important that we bring a sense of self-compassion to these new insights. Beating ourselves up, judging ourselves as bad or wrong, can generate a type of self-hatred that is both harmful and unhelpful. After learning the skill to place our attention on moment-by-moment experience, we practice using the skill in the emotionally charged context of conflict.

Next, we learn to name or note what is arising in our experience so we can discover patterns in our thinking, emotions, and bodies as we respond to life in general and conflict in particular. We explore answers to the questions: What stories do we tell ourselves about the other person or people involved in the conflict? Are others usually the ones to blame? What do we think about ourselves? What emotions habitually arise in conflict—fear, anger, disdain? Conflict and these kinds of emotions are stressful. How do our bodies register this stress, with a fight-flight-freeze response, for example? Naming helps us get more specific with our awareness practice. The practice also helps reinforce present moment awareness by arresting the mind's wandering. Naming also calms emotions and builds emotion regulation skills.

Third, we accept the reality that is in front of us just as it is. Many people's first response to conflict is resistance. They are unwilling to accept being a part of conflict, which may be one of the most challenging aspects of successfully engaging with it. This resistance and aversion most often express themselves as fearing and avoiding conflict.

Increasing the capacity to accept unpleasant and difficult experiences is helpful in all areas of life and is crucial when the experience is conflict. Being able to accept unpleasant or difficult experiences reduces our suffering and increases our equanimity and well-being. Resistance does the opposite and hampers our ability to live and work skillfully.

The fourth and fifth steps focus on body processes that play a vital role in determining whether something in the environment is a threat and preparing us to respond to it with the fight-flight-freeze response. When the body is revved up to fight, flee, or freeze, attention centers on the threat and escaping or fighting it, or freezing in the face of it; cognitive and problem-solving processes fall into the background. The practices of pausing and breathing engage a relaxation response. Pausing and breathing are self-regulatory practices that quiet physical, emotional, and mental stress and calm the body.

Seeing, naming, accepting, pausing, and breathing create space for choosing actions in response to conflict that align with one's values and goals. Making decisions and finding a path through events that are consistent with one's values and goals is the essence of wise action.

Take a look at the Mindfulness in Conflict Wheel in the following figure.

The wheel summarizes a process that enables you to see and name what you are feeling. Using mindfulness, we pay attention to bodily sensations, thoughts, and feelings. These three facets of experience align with three domains: physiological functioning, cognitive and executive functioning, and emotional functioning. These domains are arranged in a wheel because you experience bodily sensations, thoughts, and feelings at the same time. They all happen at once.

Awareness and acceptance of these domains enable us to stop, take a breath, and pause. Seeing and naming what we are feeling places our emotions in a context and enable us to exist in a grounded state, rather than an overwhelmed state. Using self-awareness, perception, and understanding together, we engage with self-management processes and support flexibility and adaptability.

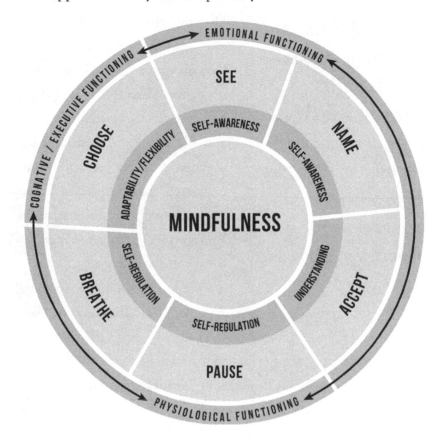

Using a mindfulness approach to become more skillful at managing conflict is not a one-and-done proposition. It requires willingness to be curious and open and a commitment to practice.

A few years ago, I was giving a presentation to a large group of project managers from all sorts of organizations. In one hour, I tried to convey all that I said in this book. Although I did some research before the presentation, I must confess that I still didn't know a tremendous amount about the work lives of project managers. During that one hour with them, it became clear that they were hungry to learn more effective ways for dealing with conflict, which was a clear and present hazard. The standing ovation as I concluded showed how much the presentation resonated with these managers. During the networking that followed this presentation, a poised fortyish woman named Julia came up to me. She explained how she had been practicing mindfulness for a while and how it helped her manage a recent conflict. Julia explained that she was a senior civilian working in the navy at the Pentagon and that she was matrixed to a team where she nominally reported to a marine corps colonel.

> *Using a mindfulness approach to become more skillful at managing conflict is not a one-and-done proposition. It requires willingness to be curious and open and a commitment to practice.*

Officially, she reported to a different boss. The colonel and her boss weren't seeing eye-to-eye about project execution, and Julia was stuck in the middle. One day in a Pentagon hallway, the colonel publicly and loudly berated Julia. While I listened to Julia describing the confrontation, it seemed to me the colonel was fully hijacked by his fight response and emotions. I wondered, "What did Julia do? How did she respond?"

Julia said that she was able to see in that moment that the colonel was in a lot of distress. She also saw, she said, that this was not really her problem but a problem between her boss and the colonel. She tuned into her breath and regulated her breathing. She noticed what was happening in her body; she felt parched from coughing due to a cold and itchy throat. As people scurried to their offices to avoid getting caught up in this scene, Julia stood in the conflagration without getting consumed. She didn't feel overly excited or provoked into rash reaction. Later that day, the colonel stopped by Julia's office to apologize for his behavior.

In recounting this event, Julia attributed her ability not to fall apart or engage unskillfully with the colonel to her regular mindfulness practice.

Incorporating a mindfulness approach doesn't mean turning yourself into yet one more self-improvement construction project. With increased awareness of the opportunities inherent in conflict, we can incorporate these challenges into our already-existing developmental path.[1]

Conflict presents us with opportunities for learning and growth as well as an occasion for suffering. Indeed, many spiritual teachers and practices suggest that when things are going well, we humans are not as interested in developing ourselves. Without challenges, we turn our attention toward distractions and amusements. Why should we take up the challenging work of training and developing our minds when life is easy?

By taking its troubles, challenges, and misfortunes onto our developmental path, conflict can become something much more than just another employee management issue. Rather, conflict creates an occasion to use crises as a pathway for a much greater, more meaningful, and visionary solutions to work problems. Conflict can help managers revamp, forge, improve, and reengineer organizational systems, frameworks, and structures. It can help you reshape the way employees relate to one another, communicate with one another, and be in relationship with one another and their clients, as suggested by the After paradigm.

Managing the Self in Conflict— AFTER

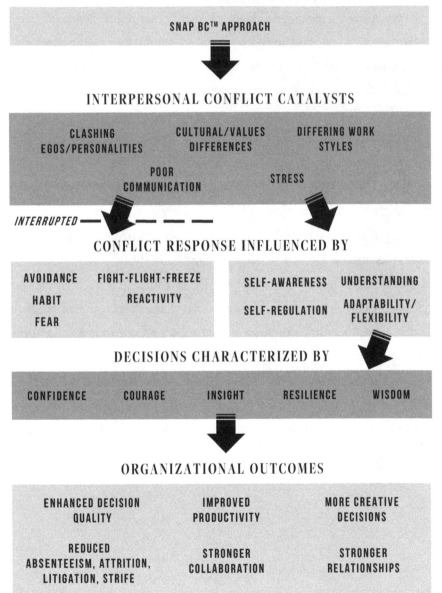

PREPARATION

SNAP BC™ APPROACH

INTERPERSONAL CONFLICT CATALYSTS

| CLASHING EGOS/PERSONALITIES | CULTURAL/VALUES DIFFERENCES | DIFFERING WORK STYLES |
| POOR COMMUNICATION | STRESS | |

INTERRUPTED

CONFLICT RESPONSE INFLUENCED BY

AVOIDANCE	FIGHT-FLIGHT-FREEZE	SELF-AWARENESS	UNDERSTANDING
HABIT	REACTIVITY	SELF-REGULATION	ADAPTABILITY/ FLEXIBILITY
FEAR			

DECISIONS CHARACTERIZED BY

| CONFIDENCE | COURAGE | INSIGHT | RESILIENCE | WISDOM |

ORGANIZATIONAL OUTCOMES

| ENHANCED DECISION QUALITY | IMPROVED PRODUCTIVITY | MORE CREATIVE DECISIONS |
| REDUCED ABSENTEEISM, ATTRITION, LITIGATION, STRIFE | STRONGER COLLABORATION | STRONGER RELATIONSHIPS |

This book and the SNAP BC approach present a knowledge path. By walking that path, I hope you will come to view and address conflict with greater confidence and less fear, with greater courage and less angst. May your journey on this path help you achieve happiness and success in managing conflict and in life.

ABOUT THE AUTHOR

Phillis is the founder of and principal consultant for Resilient At Work (R@W), a training and consulting firm that helps organizations address the behaviors that contribute to workplace conflict, high stress, and bias, all of which undermine vibrant, inclusive, and productive teams. R@W uses workplace-centric, mindfulness-based programs that have been shown to produce double-digit improvements in areas such as stress management, performance, focus and clarity, strengthened working relationships, and overall well-being.

Phillis is a NATO Medal recipient, employment lawyer, executive coach, meditation teacher and yogi. As strategic advisor, she has worked with CEOs, Cabinet secretaries, military generals, senior executive service members, managers, frontline supervisors, and employees. She has been an adjunct professor and visiting lecturer at universities around the world and has held leadership positions in the American Bar Association concerning well-being and diversity, equity, and inclusion. She is the author of numerous publications, including *The Federal Labor Relations Manual: Your Guide to Navigating the Law,* a leading treatise used by labor relations professionals throughout the federal government.

Phillis's work is influenced by more than three decades of experience working in conflict and high-stress environments including Afghanistan, Uganda, and Nepal, and defending the federal government's largest employers, as well as Fortune 100 companies, in hundreds of legal actions with billions of dollars and reputations at risk. It is also informed by years of study in Eastern philosophy, meditation, and yogic practice and training with masters in Thailand and India. Having worked with the practices and the wisdom derived from them for many years, Phillis is confident that mindfulness will help workers at every organizational level gain real-time insight into their thinking and behavior, which is so often unconscious, reactionary, and problem generating. With this insight, workers can begin to more effectively cultivate wise and compassionate workplaces, combat conflict and bias, and reduce litigation risk for their organizations. In fact, thirty-plus years of scientific research on mindfulness has confirmed its beneficial effects across a number of domains, including wellness, employee engagement, conflict management, performance, and team building.

Phillis is committed to working with organizations and individuals in ways that seek to shift thinking so that a process of integrated, sustained development can occur.

To learn more about Resilient At Work's mindfulness programs for conflict management, leadership, bias, and stress reduction, go to www.resilientatwork.com or email phillis@resilientatwork.com.

OUR SERVICES

At Resilient At Work, we specialize in workplace-centric, mindfulness-based programs which have been shown to produce double-digit improvements in areas such as stress management, performance, focus and clarity, strengthened working relationships, and overall well-being. Our organizational development strategies help to reduce stress, lessen conflict and bias, promote respect, and develop more attuned leaders.

DEVELOPMENTAL AREAS WE SPECIALIZE IN:

- Employee Stress Management
- Conflict Management
- Respect, Civility, and Bias
- Leadership Development

We marry the insight that comes from mindfulness practice to new doings based on the best research so that a process of integrated, sustained development can occur. We believe that insight without action is simply philosophy and that action without insight is foolhardy. You need both.

Here's what our clients say about what they learn and what they will do differently after working with us:

NEW LEARNINGS

» I learned that other people are just like me

» I learned I need to expand the group of people I give opportunities to—in order to guard against bias against my own group

» The "human like me" exercise hit me hard

» I learned about pausing—mindfulness as a way to manage response

---

WHAT I WILL DO DIFFERENTLY

» I have begun to hold myself accountable

» I will cascade this learning with my teams

» I will start a distance mentoring program

» I will do a better job challenging the way I think

» I will get off autopilot

MY KEY TAKEAWAY

» I can incorporate mindfulness into my day by thinking before acting

» Slow down to better use wisdom; use more system 2 thinking

» Increase my awareness of others' perspectives

» Practice empathy more

» Take ownership when I've wronged another

» Model respect and inclusion in my own home

Want to learn more? There are a number of ways you can engage with us.

Discover the secret ingredient of conflict-competent organizations by going to our website at https://www.resilientatwork.com/offerings/ and downloading the white paper.

Connect with us on LinkedIn at https://www.linkedin.com/in/phillis-morgan-800412151/.

Email us or give us a call for a complimentary consult. We can discuss the best ways R@W can work with your organization to help you achieve your goals, whether that's by delivering a familiarization presentation, a deeper workshop, facilitating mindfulness sessions, or something else. Reach us at: phillis@resilientatwork.com.

NOTES

Introduction

1. Chubb, "Employment Practices Liability Insurance: It's only a matter of when you'll be sued by an employee." https://www.chubb.com/ca-en/_assets/documents/employment-practices-liability.pdf.

2. Patrick Mitchell, *The 2017 Hiscox Guide to Employee Lawsuits*, Hiscox, 2017. According to *The 2017 Hiscox Guide to Employee Lawsuits*, which studied a representative sample of 1,214 closed claims of small to medium-sized enterprises (those with fewer than five hundred employees), $160,000 was the average cost for claims that resulted in defense and settlement payments. Almost one-quarter (24 percent) of employment charges resulted in defense and settlement costs. One in ten small-to-midsized businesses faced an employment charge of discrimination of some kind. The average time to settle a claim was 318 days.

Chapter One

1. Viktor Frankl, *Man's Search for Meaning*, translated by Ilse Lasch (Part One) (Boston: Beacon Press, 1992).

Chapter Two

1. The Mindful Management of Self in Conflict Scale draws on the Five Facets of Mindfulness Questionnaire, developed by Ruth A. Baer, Gregory T. Smith, and Kristin B. Allen (Ruth A. Baer, Gregory T. Smith, and Kristin B. Allen. "Assessment of mindfulness by self-report: The Kentucky Inventory of Mindfulness Skills." *Assessment*, 11 (2004): 191–206; Ruth A. Baer, Gregory T. Smith, Emily Lykins, Daniel Button, Jennifer Krietemeyer, Shannon Sauer, Erin Walsh, Danielle Duggan, and J. Mark G. Williams. "Construct Validity of the Five Facet Mindfulness Questionnaire in Meditating and Nonmeditating Samples." *Assessment* 15, no. 3 (September 2008): 329–42. https://doi.org/10.1177/1073191107313003); the Mindful Attention Awareness Scale, developed by Kirk Warren Brown and Richard M. Ryan (Kirk W. Brown, and Richard M. Ryan. "The benefits of being present: Mindfulness and its role in psychological well-being." *Journal of Personality and Social Psychology*, 84 (2003): 822–848); and the Cognitive Flexibility Scale, developed by Matthew M. Martin and Rebecca B. Rubin (Matthew M. Martin and Rebecca B. Rubin. "A new measure of cognitive flexibility." *Psychological Reports,* 76, no. 2 (1995): 623–626. https://doi.org/10.2466/pr0.1995.76.2.623).

2. Matthew M. Martin and Rebecca B. Rubin. A new measure of cognitive flexibility. *Psychological Reports,* 76, no. 2, (1995): 623–626. https://doi.org/10.2466/pr0.1995.76.2.623.

Chapter Three

1. Matthew Killingsworth and Daniel T. Gilbert, "A Wandering Mind Is an Unhappy Mind," *Science*, 330 (November 12, 2010): 932.

2. Kalina Christoff, "Undirected Thought: Neural Determinants and Correlates," *Brain Research*, 1428 (January 5, 2012): 51–59, https://doi.org/10.1016/j.brainres.2011.09.060.

3. Alva Noë, "Why Do Our Minds Wander?" *Cosmos & Culture*, npr.org, June 17, 2016, https://www.npr.org/sections/13.7/2016/06/17/481977 405/why-do-our-minds-wander.

4. Killingsworth and Gilbert, "A Wandering Mind Is an Unhappy Mind."

5. Killingsworth and Gilbert, "A Wandering Mind Is an Unhappy Mind."

6. Gil Fronsdal, "Mental Noting," *Insight Meditation Center*, https://www. insightmeditationcenter.org/books-articles/mental-noting/.

7. Fronsdal, "Mental Noting."

8. The general outline of this exercise, and the exercises in the chapters that follow, is identical to the structure set up in the Basic Mindful Awareness Exercise, which appears in Chapter 2.

9. Gallup, *2018 Global Emotions*, https://www.gallup.com/analytics/241961/ gallup-global-emotions-report-2018.aspx.

10. Peter J. Jordan and Ashlea C. Troth, "Managing Emotions During Team Problem Solving: Emotional Intelligence and Conflict Resolution," *Human Performance* 17, no. 2 (April 2004): 195–218, DOI: 10.1207/ s15327043hup1702_4.

11. Stephanie West Allen, "Be Mindful and Name that Feeling," *Mediate.com* (September 2013), https://www.mediate.com/articles/ WestSbl20130927.cfm; based on "When Labeling an Emotion Quiets It," by Tom Valeo, first published by the Dana Foundation, https://dana. org/.

12. Matthew D. Lieberman, Naomi I. Eisenberger, Molly J. Crockett, Sabrina M. Tom, Jennifer H. Pfeifer, and Baldwin M. Way, "Putting feelings into words: affect labeling disrupts amygdala activity in response to affective stimuli," *Psychological Science* 18 (May 2007): 421–428, DOI: 10.1111/j.1467-9280.2007.01916.x.

13. Marshall B. Rosenberg, *Nonviolent Communication: A Language of Life*, 3rd ed. (Encinitas, CA: PuddleDancer Press, 2015): 42.

Chapter Four

1. Peter Michaelson, *Why We Suffer: A Western Way to Understand and Let Go of Unhappiness* (Independently Published, 2017).

2. Jack Kornfield, *Bringing Home the Dharma, Awakening Right Where You Are* (Boston: Shambhala Publications, 2011).

3. Tim Burkett, *Nothing Holy about It: The Zen of Being Just Who You Are* (Boston: Shambhala Publications, 2015).

4. Tina Fossella, "Human Nature, Buddha Nature: An Interview with John Welwood," *Tricycle*, Spring 2011, https://tricycle.org/magazine/human-nature-buddha-nature/.

5. Alcoholics Anonymous World Services, *Alcoholics Anonymous*, 3rd ed. (New York: Alcoholics Anonymous World Services, 1976), 449–451.

6. Bhante Henepola Gunaratana, *Mindfulness in Plain English* (Sommerville, MA: Wisdom Publications) 19.

7. Thich Nhat Hahn, (Hanh, 2003), 148.

8. Thich Nhat Hanh, (2000), 84.

9. Steven Southwick and Dennis Charney, *Resilience, the Science of Mastering Life's Greatest Challenges*, 2nd ed. (New York: Cambridge University Press, 2018), 231.

10. Roxane Cohen Silver, E. Alison Holman, and Daniel N. McIntosh, "Nationwide Longitudinal Study of Psychological Responses to September 11," *Journal of the American Medical Association* 288, no. 10 (September 11, 2002): 1235–1244.

11. It's best not to choose conflict with parents and spouses for this exercise.

12. Southwick and Charney, *Resilience, the Science of Mastering Life's Greatest Challenges*, 2nd ed., 234 citing Park et al., 1996; Southwick et al., 2016.

13. Southwick and Charney, *Resilience, the Science of Mastering Life's Greatest Challenges*, 2nd ed., 234, citing Tedeschi, Park and Calhoun, 1998; Anderson and Anderson, 2003.

14. Southwick and Charney, *Resilience, the Science of Mastering Life's Greatest Challenges*, 2nd ed., 245.

15. Domyo Burk, "Letting Go of Resistance and Not Taking Everything So Personally," *The Zen Studies Podcast*, Episode 13, "What Zen 'Acceptance' and 'Non-attachment' Really Are," (May 4, 2017), https://zenstudiespodcast.com/zenacceptance/, accessed January 3, 2020.

Chapter Five

1. UCSB Science Line, "How Fast Do Nerves Send Signals to and From the Brain," February 6, 2009, http://scienceline.ucsb.edu/getkey.php?key=1950; Geraldine Kress and Steven Mennerick, "Action Potential Initiation and Propagation: Upstream Influences on Neurotransmission," *Neuroscience* 158, no. 1 (January 12, 2009): 221–222, https://www.ncbi.nlm.nih.gov/pmc/articles/PMC2661755/, doi:10.1016/j.neuroscience.2008.03.021.

2. Mike Dash, "The Story of the WWI Christmas Truce," *SmithsonianMag.com*, December 23, 2011, https://www.smithsonianmag.com/history/the-story-of-the-wwi-christmas-truce-11972213/.

3. World Health Organization, "Health as a Bridge for Peace—HUMANITARIAN CEASE-FIRES PROJECT," *Humanitarian Health Action* (blog), https://www.who.int/hac/techguidance/hbp/cease_fires/en/.

4. Council on Foreign Relations, "Global Conflict Tracker," https://www. cfr.org/global-conflict-tracker/?category=usConflictStatus; Asli Ozcelik Olcay, "'Corona Ceasefires': An Opportunity for Negotiated Agreements?" *Just Security* (May 4, 2020), https://www.justsecurity.org/69979/ corona-ceasefires-an-opportunity-for-negotiated-agreements/.

5. David Orenstein, "MIT scientists discover fundamental rule of brain plasticity," *MIT News*, June 22, 2018, https://news.mit.edu/2018/ mit-scientists-discover-fundamental-rule-of-brain-plasticity-0622.

6. Bryan E. Robinson, "The 90-Second Rule That Builds Self-Control," *Psychology Today*, (April 26, 2020), https://www.psychologytoday.com/us/ blog/the-right-mindset/202004/the-90-second-rule-builds-self-control; Jill Bolte Taylor, *My Stroke of Insight: A Brain Scientist's Personal Journey* (New York: Penguin Books, 2009).

Chapter Six

1. Kenneth Acha, MD, "Fight, Flight, Freeze Response to Stress & Conflict Resolution," *KennethMD: Prescriptions for Greatness* (blog), accessed June 9, 2020, https://www.kennethmd.com/ fight-flight-freeze-response-to-stress-conflict-resolution/.

2. Columbia University Irving Medical Center, "Bone, not adrenaline, drives fight or flight response," *Science Daily*, (September 12, 2019), https:// www.sciencedaily.com/releases/2019/09/190912111018.htm; Julian Meyer Berger, Parminder Singh, Lori Khrimian, et al., "Mediation of the Acute Stress Response by the Skeleton," *Cell Metabolism*, Volume 30, Issue 5, 2019; DOI: 10.1016/j.cmet.2019.08.012.

3. Diane Musho Hamilton, "Calming Your Brain During Conflict," *Harvard Business Review, Managing Yourself* (blog), December 22, 2015, https:// hbr.org/2015/12/calming-your-brain-during-conflict.

4. Susanne Vogel and Lars Schwabe, "Learning and Memory Under Stress: Implications for the Classroom," *NPJ: Science of Learning*, 1, 16011 (2016), https://doi.org/10.1038/npjscilearn.2016.11.

5. Diane Musho Hamilton, "Calming Your Brain During Conflict."

6. Diane Musho Hamilton, "Calming Your Brain During Conflict."

7. Mark Shwartz, "Robert Sapolsky Discusses Physiological Effects of Stress," *Stanford Report*, March 7, 2007, https://news.stanford.edu/news/2007/march7/sapolskysr-030707.html and Robert Sapolsky, *Why Zebras Don't Get Ulcers*, 3rd edition (New York: Holt Paperbacks, 2007).

8. Kate Murphy, "Outsmarting Our Primitive Responses to Fear," *The New York Times*, October 26, 2017, https://www.nytimes.com/2017/10/26/well/live/fear-anxiety-therapy.html.

9. Andrea Zaccaro, Andrea Piarulli, Marco Laurino, Erika Garbella, Danilo Menicucci, Bruno Neri, and Angelo Gemignani, "How Breath-Control Can Change Your Life: A Systematic Review on Psycho-Physiological Correlates of Slow Breathing." *Frontiers in Human Neuroscience* 12 (September 2018): 353, https://doi.org/10.3389/fnhum.2018.00353; H. J. Tsai, Terry B. J. Kuo, Guo-She Lee, and Cheryl C. H. Yang, "Efficacy of Paced Breathing for Insomnia: Enhances Vagal Activity and Improves Sleep Quality," *Psychophysiology* 52, no. 3 (March 2015): 388–396, https://doi.org/10.1111/psyp.12333; Ravinder Jerath, Molly W. Crawford, Vernon A. Barnes, and Kyler Harden, "Self-Regulation of Breathing as a Primary Treatment for Anxiety," *Applied Psychophysiology and Biofeedback* 40, no. 2 (April 2015): 107–115, https://doi.org/10.1007/s10484-015-9279-8; Anselm Doll, Britta K. Hölzel, Satja Mulej Bratec, Christine C. Boucard, Xiyao Xie, Afra M. Wolschläger, and Christian Sorg, "Mindful Attention to Breath Regulates Emotions via Increased Amygdala-Prefrontal Cortex Connectivity," *NeuroImage* 134 (July 2016): 305–313, doi:10.1016/j.neuroimage.

10. Margaret Emory, "Tracking the Mind-Body Connection: An Interview with Dr. Herbert Benson," *BrainWorld*, *Education* (blog), November 7, 2019, https://brainworldmagazine.com/tracking-mind-body-connection-interview-dr-herbert-benson/.

11. Roderik J. S. Gerritsen and Guido P. H. Band, "Breath of Life: The Respiratory Vagal Stimulation Model of Contemplative Activity," *Frontiers in Human Neuroscience* 12 (October 9, 2018), doi:10.3389/fnhum.2018.00397.

Chapter Seven

1. Robin Banck Taylor, "EEOC FY 2019 Statistics Released: Charges of Discrimination Are at an All-Time Low But the Percentage of Retaliation Charges Continues to Rise," *Workplace Blog* (blog), Butler|Snow, February 5, 2020, https://www.butlersnow.com/2020/02/eeoc-fy-2019-statistics-released-charges-of-discrimination-are-at-an-all-time-low-but-the-percentage-of-retaliation-charges-continues-to-rise/.

2. Dilip V. Jeste, Monika Ardelt, Dan Blazer, Helena C. Kraemer, George Vaillant, and Thomas W. Meeks, "Expert Consensus on Characteristics of Wisdom: A Delphi Method Study," *The Gerontologist* 50, no. 5 (October 2010): 668-680, https://doi.org/10.1093/geront/gnq022.

3. Ikujiro Nonaka and Hirotaka Takeuchi, "The Wise Leader," *The Big Idea: Ethics* (blog), *Harvard Business Review*, https://hbr.org/2011/05/the-big-idea-the-wise-leader; Mike Thompson, "What Does Wise Leadership Mean?" *Viewpoint: Leadership* (blog), IEDP Developing Leaders, April 15, 2013, https://www.iedp.com/articles/what-does-wise-leadership-mean/.

Chapter Eight

1. Prior to the twenty-first century, conventional belief was that our brains were fixed by the time we reached adulthood. Researchers thought that our brains were, in effect, static in form and function. Tremendous advances

in technology mean scientists have better tools with which to study the brain. Contemporary research reveals that our brains continue to develop well into our adult years, changing in response to experience. This is neuroplasticity, the ability of the brain to modify its structures and neural mechanisms in response to new demands placed on it by the external environment. Plasticity can occur as a result of learning, experience, and memory formation, as a result of damage to the brain, or even as a result of thought. What actually changes are the strength of connections between neurons that are engaged together in brain patterns. The more you repeat something, the more connections are made. Learning how to manage a team, brew beer, or be more mindful in conflict are all skills that we can develop and hone even as adults.

Takeaway Exercises

You can also find more helpful resources at www.resilientatwork.com.

Mindful Management of Self in Conflict Scale

1	2	3	4	5
Strongly Agree	Agree	Neither Agree or Disagree	Disagree	Strongly Disagree

	1	2	3	4	5
I could be experiencing some feeling or emotion and not be conscious of it until sometime later.	○	○	○	○	○
I criticize myself for the thoughts I'm thinking.	○	○	○	○	○
I can communicate an idea in many different ways.	○	○	○	○	○
When I experience uncomfortable bodily sensations, I feel calm soon after conflict is over.	○	○	○	○	○
I judge uncomfortable bodily sensations as bad or inappropriate.	○	○	○	○	○
I am willing to work at creative solutions to the problem.	○	○	○	○	○
I notice sensations happening in my body.	○	○	○	○	○
	1	2	3	4	5

I experience uncomfortable
sensations in my body.
○ ○ ○ ○ ○

I pause without immediately
reacting.
○ ○ ○ ○ ○

I am willing to listen and consider
alternatives for handling a problem.
○ ○ ○ ○ ○

I notice distressing thoughts or
images I am having.
○ ○ ○ ○ ○

I criticize myself for having
inappropriate emotions.
○ ○ ○ ○ ○

I have the self-confidence necessary
to try different ways of behaving.
○ ○ ○ ○ ○

I criticize myself for the feelings
I'm having.
○ ○ ○ ○ ○

	1	2	3	4	5

I am able to have distressing
thoughts or images without getting
taken over by them.
○ ○ ○ ○ ○

It seems I am "running on
automatic" without much awareness
of what I'm doing.
○ ○ ○ ○ ○

TOTAL: _____

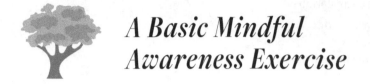

A Basic Mindful Awareness Exercise

Before you practice the exercise, read the entire section.

WHAT YOU'LL NEED

- Ten minutes when you are not too tired, sleepy, or distracted by life events to concentrate

- A relatively quiet space

- A timer

- A comfortable chair or cushion to sit on

THE POSTURE

On a chair or a cushion on the floor, sit in a position so that your body is grounded, balanced, comfortable, and alert. Imagine yourself as a king or queen on the throne preparing to receive subjects. If sitting on a chair, put your feet flat on the floor or some other stable object. If sitting on a cushion, cross your legs. Let the buttocks be balanced and firmly connected with whatever is underneath them. Lift the spine up all the way through the crown of the head, as if a string connected your parts from the sitting bones all the way up the spine to the top of the head. Dip the chin slightly toward the chest, as if holding an orange. Let the shoulders and arms be loose and relaxed. Place your hands on your thighs or lap.

INTENTION AND AIM: NO GOALS

As with other forms of contemplative practice, such as yoga, it is helpful to set an intention for the mindfulness session. When we set an intention, we are preparing to move our minds in a certain direction. We are saying to ourselves, "I'm about to undertake a task with deliberateness and intentionality." We are urging our minds to be better prepared to stay present with the contemplative activity. When setting an intention, we are not trying to achieve some goal in the activity. For example, with mindfulness meditation, we are not trying to completely clear our minds of all thoughts. We are not trying to achieve a state of utter peace. Nor are we trying to take a mental trip to some other, better place, however we define it.

Rather, the aim of our mindfulness practice is to try to pay attention to what is happening inside of us as it happens and to do so in a nonjudging, compassionate way. So when we set an intention, it should be aligned with these aims. One intention you may want to try out is "With kindness toward myself, I sit to train and develop my mind so that I may be of greater benefit to myself and others." You should feel free to create your own intention, one that is wholesome, aligned with the aims of the practice, and not overly ambitious. Then start the timer.

THE BASIC PRACTICE

To begin, allow your body to feel relaxed. Try to generate a sense of openness or open awareness and receptivity, as if you were in the presence of a trusted teacher or loving friend.

Though your body is relaxed and open, let your mind be alert and curious, as though you were reading a page-turner of a book.

Breathe.

Turn your attention to your breathing. Focus on the place in your body where you most readily and deeply connect to your breath. For most people, this is the belly or chest. Let your breath be your anchor for this exercise.

As you breathe in, notice how the belly or chest rises as the breath moves into your body. As you breathe out, notice how the belly or chest falls as the breath leaves your body. Follow the entire breathing cycle. As you breathe in, notice the pause at the top of the breath. As you breathe out, notice the pause at the bottom of the breath. Don't try to manipulate the breath in any way, such as by consciously slowing it down or holding or retaining it. Simply observe the breath, and try to do so with gentleness and open awareness. Simply observe as you breathe in and out.

Distractions will arise. A distraction is anything that takes your attention away from your anchor—your breath. You may have a thought, hear a sound, feel some emotion, or feel something happening in your body. This is normal. We cannot stop our thoughts or any of these things from happening. Our task is to try to be aware that distractions are occurring and to do so without judging or criticizing what is arising. We try to notice when we are thinking, for example, without getting entangled in the thought or story. To do this, we can say silently and gently, "Thinking"; try to let the thought flow by, like a cloud against the sky; and then return awareness to the breath.

So the exercise consists of placing our awareness on an object—our breath—trying to notice when our mind moves from that object because of distractions, and bringing our attention back to that object. We continue in this fashion until the timer sounds. If you are new to this practice, I recommend five minutes to start. If you are more experienced, set the timer to a time where you can sit comfortably without undue agitation.

When the timer sounds, slowly release your awareness of the breath. As you continue to breathe, let yourself become aware of your body on the chair or cushion and your presence in the environment. You can take a few deep inhalations and exhalations to encourage this return.

Now that you have read all of the instructions and have gathered what you need, you are ready to begin.

REFLECTION QUESTIONS

If you like, write responses to the following questions on the lines that follow each.

How did you find this exercise?

_____

_____

_____

_____

What was the experience of sitting still and simply watching the rise and fall, coming and going of the breath, like for you?

_____

_____

_____

_____

What did you learn, discover, or notice about your ability to pay sustained attention to a particular object—your breath?

_____

_____

_____

_____

What did you notice or learn about distractions, such as thoughts, emotions, or sounds as they occurred?

_____

_____

_____

_____

Did you become entangled in the distractions, or were you able to watch them with some level of objectivity and let them go?

_____

_____

_____

_____

What would support you in incorporating such a practice regularly in your life?

_____

_____

_____

_____

What likely obstacles would you need to address?

_____

_____

_____

_____

Mindfulness in Conflict Visualization

This mindfulness visualization begins the process of seeing how we show up in conflict. Before you begin the exercise, read the entire section.

WHAT YOU'LL NEED

- Ten minutes when you are not too tired, sleepy, or distracted by life events to concentrate

- A relatively quiet space

- A timer

- A comfortable chair or cushion to sit on

THE EXERCISE

The aim of this exercise is to maintain awareness on an object: the remembered conflict. During the exercise, you will recall the conflict in as much detail as possible—where you were, what you and others were saying and doing, and what you were thinking and feeling. Visualizing in this amount of detail can be difficult the first time you try it because your mental muscles are not well trained. Try not to judge any difficulty or worry about it. You may also find that distracting thoughts arise. That's normal. Try to be aware that a distraction occurred, and then simply bring your mind back to the remembered conflict. Again, try not to judge the distractions, get entangled in them, or worry about them. Over time as you practice, you may become more adept at noticing and handling distractions. They may even occur with less frequency.

Choose a conflict to work with. It's best to start with something simple, the same as you would work with the lightest weights at the gym if you were a beginner or had not been there for a long time. If you started with the heaviest weights, you would risk injury, discouragement, or demotivation. Similarly, avoid choosing a situation that is too overwhelming. Instead, choose a conflict that has caused you some suffering but does not inspire self-criticism, trigger self-judgment, or pose an existential threat.

THE POSTURE AND INTENTION

On a chair or a cushion on the floor, sit in a position so that your body is comfortable—not too stiff and not too loose. Set an intention for the session, for example, "With kindness toward myself, I am sitting to gain insight into my way of being during conflict so that I may be of greater benefit to myself and others." Then start the timer.

THE PRACTICE

To begin, allow your body to feel relaxed. Try to generate a sense of openness, open awareness, and receptivity, as if you were in the presence of a loving pet or trusted friend.

Let your mind be alert and curious, as though you were interested in seeing what your pet was going to do next or hearing your friend describe a trip to an exotic location. Have an intention to be present for and curious about what arises next.

Breathe.

Turn your attention to your breathing. Focus on the place in your body that you most readily and deeply connect to your breath. For most people, this is the belly, chest, or nostrils. Let your breath be your anchor. You can always return to the breath moving in and out of your body if you want to leave the visualization.

As you breathe in, attend to the feeling. Notice that you are breathing in. As you breathe out, attend to the feeling. Notice that you are breathing out. Follow the entire breathing cycle. As you breathe in, notice the pause at the top of the breath. As you breathe out, notice the pause at the bottom of the breath. Observe the breath with gentleness, presence, and open awareness, without judging or criticizing what is arising. Simply observe as you breathe in and out.

Continue following your breath until you get some sense of balance and stability, even if it is slight, fleeting, or temporary. This might take a few minutes.

Next, visualize a time when you were in conflict with someone at work. Choose a conflict of light intensity and scope. If you cannot identify a light work-related conflict, choose one from other areas of your life. To keep the intensity and scope light, avoid choosing a conflict with a parent or spouse.

Gently turn your awareness away from your breath and to the remembered conflict. Try to generate specificity around the conflict. Where were you? Who else was involved? Then try to get a sense of the conflict unfolding and your experience in it as it did. What was happening? What did you say? What did others say? What were you thinking about the conflict, the others in it? What emotions did you experience? What was the body language like, your demeanor? Try to see yourself and others as clearly as possible in the conflict. Don't worry if the details are difficult to visualize. Even if you cannot see the event clearly, see if you can get a feeling for the tone of the experience, similar to how you feel when you awaken from a vivid dream.

As you do this exercise, try to refrain from judging or criticizing your experience. Like you would with a dear friend in distress, just be with yourself with care and compassion. If judgments or criticism arise, just note that you are thinking, and return to your breath and memory.

Continue remembering the conflict, along with its details, until the timer sounds. Just try to watch and be with it as the drama unfolds, with yourself as one of the main players.

When the timer sounds, slowly release your awareness of the conflict, and gently turn your attention back to your breath and the present moment. Continue following your breath, and let yourself become aware of your surroundings. You can inhale deeply and exhale deeply to help return your awareness to the present.

Without entanglement or fanfare, allow yourself to feel a sense of accomplishment, much as you would for successfully undertaking a challenge.

Now that you have read all of the instructions and have gathered what you need, you are ready to begin.

REFLECTION QUESTIONS

If you like, write responses to the following questions on the lines that follow each.

How did you feel about this exercise?

What was the experience of sitting still and simply replaying the conflict in your mind like for you?

_____

_____

_____

_____

Did you discover anything about how you showed up in the conflict you visualized?

_____

_____

_____

_____

How easy or difficult was it to refrain from judging or criticizing thoughts as you let the conflict unfold in your mind?

_____

_____

_____

_____

What did you learn, discover, or notice about the conflict itself?

_____

_____

_____

_____

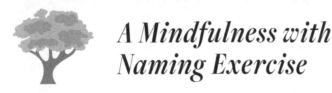

A Mindfulness with Naming Exercise

For this exercise, you will need a timer, chair or cushion, and relatively quiet space.

Read the instructions in their entirety before beginning the exercise.

After reading the instructions, sit in a comfortable position, and place your timer within arm's reach. And when ready, if you are new to mindfulness, set the timer for five minutes.

Set an intention for the mindfulness session that moves you in a positive direction. For example, "With kindness toward myself, I am sitting to gain insight into my way of being during conflict so that I may be of greater benefit to myself and others." Then start the timer.

Allow your body to relax. Try to generate a sense of open awareness and receptivity, as if you were in the presence of a loving pet or a trusted friend.

Let your mind be alert and curious, as though you were interested in seeing what your dog would do next or hearing your friend describe her trip to an exotic location. Generate an energetic intention that you will be present for whatever arises in the next five minutes.

Turn your attention to your breathing. Focus on the place in your body where you most readily and deeply connect to your breath. Let your breath be your anchor, the place you return to whenever your attention is drawn away.

As you breathe in, know that you are breathing in. As you breathe out, know that you are breathing out. Pay attention throughout the breathing cycle. As you breathe in, notice the pause at the top of the breath; as you breathe out, notice the pause at the bottom of the breath.

Observe your breath with a gentle, present, open awareness. Simply observe what arises without judging or criticizing. Like a curious baby exploring the world, generate a sense of nonjudging, open curiosity.

Thoughts, emotions, sounds, smells, sights, or bodily sensations will draw your attention away from your breath. This is normal. The key is to try to notice the moment when your attention is being drawn away. Often it can take several seconds or even minutes before we notice our focus is no longer on our object of attention. So it is a significant achievement when we are able to notice this pulling away of our attention.

When something draws your attention away, name the sensation, such as "thinking," "feeling," "hearing" "smelling," or "sensing" silently and softly, like a gentle nudge. Naming is not forceful or accusatory. Try not to get entangled in stories you might want to tell about what you're experiencing. Simply name the experience and then return your awareness back home, to your breath. Repeat this process every time your mind wanders from attention to your breathing.

Continue in this way until the timer sounds. Then, slowly release your focus on naming, and gently turn your attention back to your breath, back to the present moment, back to your surroundings. You can deeply inhale and exhale to encourage this return to the present.

Now, without entanglement or fanfare, allow yourself to feel a sense of accomplishment, much as you would for successfully undertaking some challenge.

REFLECTION QUESTIONS

How did you find this exercise?

How easy or difficult was it to become aware that a distraction had occurred?

_____

_____

_____

_____

How did naming affect your experience with the distracting event?

_____

_____

_____

_____

Were you able to notice any storytelling that may have accompanied the naming?

_____

_____

_____

_____

How easy or difficult was it to refrain from judging, evaluating, or criticizing your experience?

_____

_____

_____

_____

Feelings Wheel for Identifying and Naming Emotions

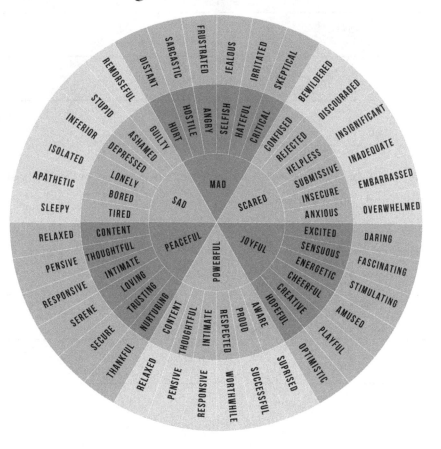

Source: Gloria Wilcox, "The Feeling Wheel: A Tool for Expanding Awareness of Emotions and Increasing Spontaneity and Intimacy," Transactional Analysis Journal 12, no. 4 (December 2017): 274-276, https://doi. org/10.1177/036215378201200411.

Naming Strong Emotions in a Conflict Visualization

In the preceding naming exercise, you may have been surprised to see how active the senses are and how easily they can capture our interest, taking our minds away from what we are doing. As you continue to work with these practices—what I call mental strength training—you will develop stronger mental muscles for paying attention to exactly what you want to, without the mind being so easily pulled away. Even after years of practice, as I have gained some facility at stilling the mind, I continue to marvel at how the still mind allows me to observe the never-ending, life-sustaining processes occurring in my body and mind—heart beating, mind thinking, pain coming and going, breath circulating, sounds rising and falling, and so much more. With so much happening with the senses, I find that focusing on one thing in my formal practice can help promote concentration and deepen insight. This is what we will do in this exercise.

Being emotionally charged is a strong indicator that conflict is afoot. And the inability to manage strong emotions, especially fear, is one of the principal responses that severely weakens our ability to be more skillful in conflict. For that reason, in this exercise we will work with naming strong emotions. By doing so, we will begin to awaken and familiarize ourselves with our emotional responses to conflict as well as build the skills to tame them.

To begin, prepare as you would in the Mindfulness with Naming exercise. Bring your awareness to the place in your body where you most readily and deeply connect to your breath. Continue in this way until you get a sense of stability, even if slight, fleeting, or temporary. This might take a few minutes.

Next, visualize a time when you were in conflict with someone at work. As before, choose a conflict of light intensity and scope. If you cannot identify a work-related conflict, choose one from another area of your life. Choose a conflict that has caused you some difficulty, but one that is not too overwhelming.

Gently turn your awareness away from your breath and to the remembered conflict. As before, try to generate as much specificity as you can around the conflict. Try to recall where the conflict arose. Without focusing on the "why," how did the conflict seem to arise? Who was involved? What happened? What did you say? What did others say? What was the body language like? Try to see yourself and others as clearly as possible in the conflict. Don't worry if the details are difficult to visualize. Even if you cannot see the event clearly, see if you can get a feeling for the tone of the experience, similar to how you feel when you awaken from a vivid dream.

Remembering the conflict and the feeling of what it was like being in it, see if you can name the strong emotions that you observed yourself feeling. As you vividly remember the conflict, what emotions are arising: fear, anger, sadness, nervousness, helplessness?

Name each emotion as it arises, as best as you can and without judging or evaluating it. For example, if you are feeling fear, name it "fear," without judging whether the fear is valid, reasonable, good, or bad. Continue to note and name each strong emotion as you observe it in the remembered conflict. If at any time the emotions seem too overwhelming, come back to your home base, which is the breath.

Continue with this exercise until the timer sounds. Then, slowly release your awareness of the conflict, and gently turn your attention back to your breath, back to the present moment, back to your surroundings. You can deeply inhale and exhale to encourage this return to the present.

Now, without entanglement or fanfare, allow yourself to feel a sense of satisfaction, much as you would after completing a challenging undertaking.

 ### REFLECTION QUESTIONS

How did you find this exercise?

_____

_____

_____

_____

Were you able to observe the emotions you experienced as you recalled the conflict?

_____

_____

_____

_____

Were you able to identify the emotions you experienced as you recalled the conflict?

_____

_____

_____

_____

How easy or difficult was it to name emotions rather than thoughts, assessments, evaluations, and the like?

_____

_____

_____

_____

Did naming have any effect on you in the present moment as you remembered the conflict?

_____

_____

_____

_____

How easy or difficult was it to refrain from judging, evaluating, or criticizing your experience?

_____

_____

_____

_____

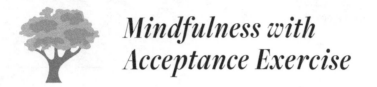

Mindfulness with Acceptance Exercise

For this exercise, you will need some time when you are not too tired, sleepy, or distracted by life to concentrate, a timer placed within arm's reach, a chair or cushion, and a relatively quiet space.

Read the entire section before beginning.

After reading the instructions, sit on a chair, a cushion, or on the floor in a position so that your body is grounded, balanced, comfortable, and alert. When ready, if you are new to mindfulness, set the timer for five minutes.

Set an intention for the session to pay attention to what is happening inside, as it happens, in a nonjudging, compassionate way. For example, you might state your intention as, "With kindness toward myself, I am sitting to gain insight into my way of showing up with respect to accepting conflict so that I may be of greater benefit to myself and others." Feel free to create your own intention that is wholesome, not overly ambitious, and aligned with the aims of the practice. Then start the timer.

Allow your body to feel relaxed. Try to generate a sense of open awareness and receptivity, as if you were in the presence of a trusted teacher or loving friend. Though your body is relaxed and open, let your mind be alert and curious, as though you were reading a page-turner of a book.

Turn your attention to your breathing. Focus on the place in your body where you most readily and deeply connect to your breath. For most, that's the belly or chest. Let your breath be your anchor.

As you breathe in, notice how the belly or chest rises as the breath moves into your body. As you breathe out, notice how the belly or chest falls as the breath leaves your body. Follow the entire breathing cycle. As you breathe in, notice the pause at the top of the breath; as you breathe out, notice the pause at the bottom of the breath. Don't manipulate the breath by consciously slowing it down or holding it. Simply observe your breath with a gentle, present, open awareness. With gentleness and open awareness, simply observe as you breathe in and out.

Continue observing your breath until you get some sense of steadiness or stability, even if slight or fleeting. This might take a few minutes.

Next, as in previous exercises, visualize a time when you were in a work-related conflict with someone. The conflict should not be of great intensity or scope. If you cannot identify a work-related conflict, choose one from another area of your life. Whether work-related or from some other area of life, choose a conflict that has caused you some suffering but does not pose an existential threat.

After you have the conflict in mind, gently turn your awareness away from your breath and to the remembered conflict. Be as specific as you can in recalling the details of the conflict. Where did the conflict take place? Whom were you with? How did the conflict arise? How is it unfolding? What are you saying? What are others saying? What is the tone and body language like? Try to see yourself and others as clearly as possible in the conflict. If this visualization is difficult, do not worry about it. Try to generate a feeling of being in the conflict, even if it is amorphous. Even if you cannot see the event clearly, see if you can get a feel for the tone of the experience.

Now, remembering the conflict as vividly as you can and having some feeling of what it was like being in it, using the naming technique that you learned in the last chapter, name the strong emotions that arise. For example, if you are feeling hatred toward the other person, name it "hatred." Is it fear? Anger? Overwhelm? Inadequacy? Describe what the emotion feels like. For example, perhaps it feels heavy, stuck, or hard. Where in your body do you feel this emotion the strongest? Your stomach? Chest? Shoulders? Jaw? Continue naming, describing, and locating as strong emotions arise.

If at any time they seem too overwhelming, come back to your home base, which is the breath.

Now try to get a sense of what you might be accepting or rejecting about this experience. What resistance might you be experiencing? Even if it doesn't feel strong, observe it, like a detective, to detect even the subtlest sense of rejection or pushing away. What do you want to turn away from? What feels uncomfortable? What do you find most difficult about being in the situation? See both the discomfort and the way you want to turn away from it. You are not trying to manipulate or change anything. You are just trying to get to know yourself and the way you are in conflict.

As you do this exercise, refrain from judging or criticizing your experience. Like you would with a dear friend in distress, just be with yourself with care and compassion.

Continue the exercise until the timer sounds. Then, slowly release your awareness of the conflict, and gently turn your attention back to your breath, back to the present moment, back to your surroundings. You can deeply inhale and exhale to encourage this return.

Without entanglement or fanfare, congratulate yourself as you would a dear friend for undertaking a challenging project. Out of all the things tugging at your time and attention, you chose to devote your energy to training and developing your mind, which will benefit you, your colleagues, subordinates, superiors, direct reports, and those to whom you report.

REFLECTION QUESTIONS

How did you feel about this exercise? I found this exercise:

_____

_____

_____

_____

What, if anything, felt uncomfortable? I felt most uncomfortable when:

_____

_____

_____

_____

What aspects of the conflict or your response to it did you find hard to accept? I found it hard to accept:

_____

_____

_____

_____

What stories did you tell yourself about the conflict or your response to it? I noticed I would tell stories about:

_____

_____

_____

_____

What aspects of the conflict or your response to it did you want to turn away from or resist? I noticed I resisted when:

_____

_____

_____

_____

What aspects of this exercise did you gain insight from or were surprising? I gained the most insight from or was most surprised when:

_____

_____

_____

_____

What about engaging with this exercise are you most proud of? I am most proud of myself for:

_____

_____

_____

_____

Brief, Forceful Breathing Exercise in Preparation for Conflict

Take a comfortable meditation seat with a straight spine and relaxed body, as described in previous chapters. Read the following instructions completely before you try the exercise.

No timer is necessary for this exercise. You'll complete at least three rounds of forceful breathing, more if you like.

For a few moments, bring awareness to your breathing, initially paying attention to its quality without trying to manipulate it in any way. How is your breath now? Is it smooth or choppy? Shallow or deep? Short or long? Just see what is there without creating a story about what's going on.

Next, forcefully from the belly draw in a deep breath through the nostrils. Then forcefully exhale through the nose. It is okay to make a sound as you forcefully exhale. In fact, this is encouraged to promote relaxation. Repeat at least two more times.

Now return to regular breathing for as long as you like. When you're ready, ease out of the practice altogether by slowly bringing awareness back to your surroundings and letting go of this exercise completely.

REFLECTION QUESTIONS

Is this a practice you can use in your everyday life? If so, in a few words describe how or when you could incorporate this practice.

I can use forceful breathing when

_____

_____

_____

_____

If you believe this is not a practice for you, describe why not.

_____

_____

_____

_____

I don't think forceful breathing is a practice I can use in my life because

_____

_____

_____

_____

Balanced Breathing Exercise in Preparation for Conflict

Balanced breathing is one of my favorite breathing techniques. I regularly use this technique while lying in bed before I go to sleep. With each deep exhalation, I am able to release and let go a little bit more of the stressors and cares of the day. With each inhalation, I am able to invite in a little more peace and calm. I feel noticeably more refreshed and grounded the next morning. Feel free to try it yourself before bedtime. Just let yourself go. Don't worry if you're doing it right or for how long you should do it. Let the breath relax you, providing a soothing entryway to sleep.

In balanced breathing, you breathe solely through the nose and breathe deeply from the belly. Practice as if you were in a library, church, or some other sacred space where maintaining discretion is vitally important. We practice subtly because our goal is to use the skill subtly when others are near or when we are in public.

With belly breathing—diaphragmatic or abdominal breathing— we seek to engage the diaphragm by expanding it and engage the chest less or not at all. Recall from the beginning of the chapter that the diaphragm is the respiratory muscle that sits beneath the lungs and in front of the abdominal organs. It separates the thoracic cavity of the torso from the abdominal cavity and is attached to the lower ribs, lower sternum, and the spine in the lower back.

When you are practicing alone, you can use this anatomy lesson to connect with the action of breathing. If you place one hand on the upper abdomen, you can feel the diaphragm move out during inhalations.

The lower rib cage also expands when you inhale. To connect with this sensation, place your hands along each side of the lower rib cage. With correct diaphragmatic breathing, you should notice the rib cage expanding outward.

During this exercise, your attention is partially on counting and partially on watching the expansion of the belly or rib cage (choose one) as you inhale and exhale.

Choose only one point of focus during a practice session. Do not alternate between them during a practice session, as doing so encourages distraction. Leave your hands in place for as long as you like or until you feel comfortable that you are performing the technique correctly.

Take your meditation seat, as described in previous chapters. Read the instructions completely before you begin.

No timer is necessary for this exercise.

Bring awareness to your breathing, initially paying attention to its quality without trying to manipulate it in any way. How is your breath? Is it soft or rough? Constricted or free flowing? Full or shallow? Fleeting or enduring? Just try to notice what is there without judging whether your breath is good or bad.

In balanced breathing, we are trying to maintain uniformity of the inhalations and exhalations. Each should be of equal duration and effort. Take a deep inhalation through the nose to the count of four: one, two, three, four. Then exhale through the nose to the count of four: one, two, three, four. It doesn't matter if your count is fast or slow as long as you count at the same pace for inhalations and exhalations.

Again, draw in a deep breath through the nostrils to the count of four. Notice the slight pause at the top of the breath. Now exhale through the nostrils to the count of four. Notice the slight pause at the bottom of the breath. Notice the expansion and contraction of the belly or rib cage.

If at any time feelings of anxiety or stress rise to the level of distress, or you find that counting to four is unmanageable for whatever reason, you have options. You can alter the count, always making sure the exhalation and the inhalation are the same length. Or you can release the exercise and return to a grounded space, such as simple breath awareness. You can even open your eyes to reorient and ground yourself.

Stay with this practice for as long as you like and can do so comfortably, without tension or distress. Then, take a few moments to ease out of the practice. If your eyes were partially or completely closed, slowly lift your eyelids. Notice what you see. Then begin to expand your awareness outward from narrow to wide. Show appreciation to yourself for making the effort to develop yourself. Then, see what part of the practice you can carry with you in your next endeavor or task.

 ## REFLECTION QUESTIONS

How does your body feel now?
I noticed my body feels like

_____

_____

_____

_____

What different sensations do you notice?

I noticed my sensations include

_____

_____

_____

_____

How does your mind feel?

My mind feels

_____

_____

_____

What differences in your thoughts or feeling of mental readiness do you notice?

I notice my thoughts and feelings of mental readiness are now

_____

_____

_____

_____

What shifts in your emotions do you notice?
I notice my emotions are

_____

_____

_____

_____

An Exercise to Uncover Your Personal Values

As you prepare to choose a course of action for addressing conflict, it's helpful to have a guiding light. This North Star will help guide your actions and help you check whether the way you are responding to conflict aligns with your values. A simple and effective way for uncovering your values is to make your own list of Inspirators.

Right now, pause. Take a few minutes to reflect on your heroes, those who inspire you. What qualities do they demonstrate that you connect with, that you aspire to embody? In the space below, write the name of one to three Inspirators and a few of their qualities that inspire you.

My Inspirator's Name:
What I admire:

_____

_____

_____

_____

My Inspirator's Name:
What I admire:

_____

_____

_____

_____

My Inspirator's Name:
What I admire:

_____

_____

_____

_____

As you prepare to choose a course of action for resolving conflict, check inside yourself. Ask, "How can my words and behavior align with what I value?" When harmony is the value, for example, aligned behavior may mean using words that signal shared circumstance, remind what has been overcome in the past, and express confidence that this challenge, too, will be met. Words misaligned with harmony would draw distinctions or separate you from your counterpart. Expressing harmony may mean arranging to have the conversation in a private place or in surroundings where power dynamics are not used as leverage.

An Exercise to Uncover Your Organization's Values

Organizational values may include characteristics like integrity, honesty, excellence, compassion, and accountability—the list is practically endless. Many organizations spend countless hours toiling over and wordsmithing values statements that you see on plaques hanging in the cafeteria or meeting rooms or included in email signature lines. My observation from working with teams is that putting their values, which are ordinarily invisible, opaque, or unthought of, into words is a clarifying experience. At some level, the effort to clarify what the organization cares about and what it prioritizes adds value. Putting values into words can be revelatory and may prompt some serious soul searching.

Pause again. Now consider your organization's heroes. Who does your organization consider its heroes? The people might be readily apparent in things like your organization's origin story, leaders' public statements, TED Talks, or marketing campaigns. Finding your organization's heroes may involve a bit more sleuthing, in which case you should feel free to ask colleagues. In the space below, write the names of one to three organizational heroes and a few of each one's qualities.

My organization's hero:
What my organization admires:

_____

_____

_____

_____

My organization's hero:
What my organization admires:

_____

_____

_____

_____

My organization's hero:
What my organization admires:

_____

_____

_____

_____

Notice the extent of overlap or gaps between your individual values and those of the organization.

As you know, organizations don't manifest values; people do. No amount of artful drafting can replace the experience of living your or your organization's values in day-to-day workplace interactions. If you learned after the preceding exercise that your personal values align with those of your organization, you are likely to find more organizational support for the conflict resolution strategies you adopt, whether those are taking care of employees, honesty, transparency, respect for people, professionalism, or whatever they may be.

However, if there are significant gaps between your personal values and those of the organization, it will be more difficult for you to align your conflict resolution strategies and behaviors with the values the organization says it cares about. This misalignment may present an opportunity for you to start a dialogue to explore these gaps with the aim of bringing the organization's expressed values and yours into greater alignment in the context of conflict resolution.

As you prepare to choose a course of action for resolving conflict, check inside yourself. Ask, "How can my words and behavior align with organizational values?" Where honesty and transparency are highly valued, this might mean, for example, talking about your doubts, misgivings, or biases—mind states that are not visible to your counterpart in a conflict, but which may contribute to the conflict. If respect for people is prized, this might mean intentionally behaving in ways that say, "I hear you." This respect could include deep listening skills—for example, maintaining eye contact, avoiding distractions (don't return emails or texts while talking, and turn off the phone), showing curiosity, and asking questions.